THE
HEALTHY
CAT AND DOG
COOK BOOK

Good Health

Joan Harper

This book is written for the benefit of the cats and dogs that live with you, their needs, their tastes and their good health. A large type face is used so that all eyes, young and old can read it easily and use it often. Keeping your cat and dog friends healthy and happy through a good diet is not difficult and you will be rewarded many times over.

THE HEALTHY CAT AND DOG COOK BOOK

Natural Recipes Using Nutritious, Economical Foods and Good Advice for Happier, Healthier and More Beautiful Pets.

by JOAN HARPER

A Dutton Paperback
E.P. Dutton • New York

JOAN HARPER
Box 332, Rt. 3
Richland Center, Wis. 53581

This paperback edition first published 1979 by E.P. Dutton, a Division of Elsevier-Dutton Publishing Co., Inc., New York

For information contact:
E.P. Dutton, 2 Park Avenue, New York, N.Y. 10016
Library of Congress Catalog Card Number: 79-63247

ISBN: 0-525-47586-9

Published simultaneously in Canada by
Clarke, Irwin & Company Limited, Toronto and Vancouver

10 9 8 7 6 5 4 3 2 1

To DUCHESS
who taught us much about
the ways of animals.

Illustrated by Dan Harper

TABLE OF CONTENTS

I   INTRODUCTION 7

II FOOD REQUIREMENTS OF
    DOGS AND CATS 13

III RECIPES 19
    Cutting Costs to the bone 19
    Dry Foods and Cereals 28
    Doggie want a Cracker? 38
    Beans and Soybeans 44
    Eggs and Milk Products 51
    Fish 57
    Meat Dishes 59
    Vegetables and Herbs 68
    Celebrations 73
    Recipes for Special Diets 75

IV USING COMMERCIAL
            PET FOODS 87

V   HOW TO SUPPLEMENT
            YOUR PET'S DIET 93

VI SOME NATURAL
            HOME REMEDIES 101

VII AN INCREASE IN THE FAMILY . . . 111

VIII NAMING THE NEW ONES 119

IX FURTHER NOTES AND
            DEFINITIONS 125

    BIBLIOGRAPHY 140

    INDEX 142

THE HEALTHY CAT AND DOG COOK BOOK

I INTRODUCTION

People talk about survival these days and wonder whether we should feed our pets food that could be used to keep people from starving on other continents and perhaps this one too. I am passionately in favor of feeding hungry people everywhere, and I extend this feeling to all living creatures. I am aware of nature's way of controlling human and animal populations by starvation, but I also know that nature is abundant and that starvation is only the final solution after all the other checks and balances have failed.

I do not believe that we must choose between our pets and hungry people. The problem, I think, is one of management and distribution. We use too much energy to produce our food, in most cases, ten calories of energy to get one calorie of food. If we could reverse this expenditure of energy, we would have far fewer problems.

It is true that cats and dogs require considerable protein, cats more than dogs, but this can be partly furnished from sources that people don't use anyway. Both cats and dogs also need more vegetables and whole grains than most people realize. These recipes are designed to help you care for your pets in a way that is most supportive of them, your family, and nature in general. Energy, yours and the earth's, is conserved by using leftovers and foods that might normally be discarded by you or the market, such as bones and scrap meats and fish; also by combining grains and legumes to increase the usable protein content of both.

Most important, we will bring our pets closer to the family by sharing some of our foods instead of always segregating them at mealtimes by opening cans or packages that in some instances we are reluctant to even touch. I am not against using commercial cat and dog foods as long as they are of good quality, say clearly what they contain, and do not contain additives and preservatives. However, the exclusive use of commercial foods makes for an unbalanced and unhealthy diet.

If you are now feeding a combination of commercial canned and dry food and don't feel like fussing, use these recipes for part of their daily ration and mix it all together. Be sure to read Chapter V on supplements.

I used to think cooking for pets was unnecessary and time consuming and that my cats especially would never eat what I cooked for them anyway. I still believe that most meats are best served raw or cooked as little as possible.

8

But I was pleasantly surprised to see not only our dogs, but all four cats contentedly munching on string beans, carrots, asparagus stalks and the like, as long as the vegetables were chopped small and mixed with something they liked. This mixing of foods is the best way I know to introduce new tastes. If your dog or cat absolutely refuse to eat anything new, keep trying, and if necessary, let them go hungry for a day or two. I believe it is most important to have them eating a good variety of foods, and a day or two of fasting won't hurt at all.

I have found a blender or an osterizer to be very useful, almost indispensable for a lot of these recipes. I use mine every day for something or other. If you don't have one, a good meat chopper will do, but I would suggest that if you are able to save any money with these meals, use some of it to buy a blender. You won't regret it.

9

Another thing, I have tried to keep most of these recipes simple enough for a child to prepare. Cooking for Fido or Puss might be a really good way to introduce your little one to the kitchen. The audience will probably be appreciative even of the near misses. In the beginning, you might taste the dish first to make sure it is edible.

Feeding pets seems to have become a very controversial subject indeed. There is little agreement among the experts on any aspect of a cat or dog's diet. Some nutritionists claim that an animal can live perfectly well on a chemical diet, made up of artificial food as long as all the required nutrients are present. At the other end of the spectrum is the method of feeding the animal as it would feed itself if it were living in the wilderness. Some advise a varied diet, others say animals are better off with the same foods every day as long as a complete, balanced diet is given. Some feed only raw foods, others cook everything thoroughly, some recommend that food be chopped or minced, and others insist on giving larger pieces for chewing exercise.

All agree however, that pets need plenty of fresh water at all times, that there is no good substitute for a mother animal's milk, and that regular feeding times and places be maintained.

Cats and dogs, like humans, have their own individual tastes and needs in foods, but they can also adapt to a variety of conditions. For instance, some cats live mostly on milk and dairy products, and others won't touch a drop of it. Some dogs are given milk every day and others never taste it again after they are weaned.

Cats that are finicky about food can easily become addicted to one type of food and refuse all else for days, even weeks. In fact they will almost rather starve to death than eat a diet they dislike. As they were originally desert type creatures, their bodies are very efficient at recycling water and can survive with little food for some period of time. So it is much easier to keep feeding many different kinds of food from the start, than to cope with a cat that is hooked on one kind.

You may not realize it, but cats do appreciate good flavors and the smell of warm meals. However they do not like anything that is overcooked. Being carnivores, cats and dogs have become adapted over millions of years to rather high fiber and high ash diets from eating the bones, viscera, skin and fur, as well as the muscle and stomach contents (vegetable) of their prey.

Since dogs, like tiggers, love practically everything, it is much easier to feed them a variety of things, even fruit if they like it. Apples and melons, as well as berries are relished by many dogs and some cats, too. You may catch them eating manure and even earth. Do not be alarmed by this as long as it comes from healthy cows or horses*. I would draw the line at that

*"The Complete Herbal Book of the Dog"
  by Juliette de Bairacli Levy

11

point, however. As for eating earth, puppies and other young animals probably do this because earth is a natural antibiotic. The bacteria and mold content in good clean earth can establish cultures of digestive or protective organisms in their stomachs and intestines.* This isn't all that outrageous—penicillin and other helpful molds come from the soil.

Of course you know that many dogs and most cats will run outside on a spring day and eat crab or quack grass, and then throw it up. This seems to be a beneficial procedure, although it may not look it. I admit it did give me a turn one fine spring day to see all four of my cats throwing up at once. I am told by Juliette de Bairacli Levy that the coarse rough grass contains much silica and has a scrubbing action like an internal rake. The animal thus rids itself of impurities along with bile and mucus. Sometimes a portion of the grass is digested to clean the lower part of the digestive tract and is excreted in the feces.

*"The Living Soil" by Lady Eve Balfour

II FOOD REQUIREMENTS OF DOGS AND CATS

Cats must have some animal protein every day, but dogs can be well nourished on vegetable proteins alone as long as the protein is complete. This means that all eight essential amino acids that the body cannot manufacture, must be present. Some complete vegetable proteins are brewers yeast, wheat germ, and soy beans. All other beans, peas, or legumes must be combined with a cereal or grain to yield a complete protein.

Dogs must have at least twenty per cent protein, and cats should have about thirty five per cent protein as measured by weight in dry food.

Proportions of food elements for dogs.

*20% protein
(meat, fish, eggs,
cheese, plant pro-
tein from beans,
corn, peas, etc.)*

*20% fat or oil
(meat drippings,
vegetable oils)*

*60% carbohydrates
(plant starches, wheat,
potatoes, corn, rice,
cereals, grains, etc.)*

Proportions of food elements for cats.

Cats require higher proportions of proteins and fats.

35% protein   30% fat   35% carbohydrates

Don't think you are doing your dog any favors by giving him an all meat diet! More than 30% of meat protein can bring on digestive, and other problems. I almost ruined the health of our beautiful Weimaraner, Duchess, because she seemed to prefer meat. She developed heart trouble and gained too much weight. When I cut her meat ration to one fourth and added dry cereal food, I was very much surprised to see how she slimmed down and how her health improved. Alas, she had to keep on with her heart medicine, but the addition of brewers yeast, lecithin, cod liver oil and wheat germ oil kept her spry and youthful for the rest of her life.

Fat is also needed to produce good health and beautiful shiny coats. Dogs should be given around fifteen to twenty per cent, and cats should have twenty five to thirty per cent. Part of it should be polyunsaturated oils. Outdoor dogs and cats who can run can be fed more fat, but they will need more protein to digest it.

All animals require carbohydrates as a source of energy. Whole grain cereals and flours contain most of the vitamins and minerals essential for good health. Add cereals or grains slowly to rapidly boiling water to make the starch more easily digested for dogs and cats. Dogs can handle up to sixty five per cent carbohydrates in their diet, cats should have no more than forty per cent.

Vitamins and minerals are extremely important in your pet's diet. Most of my recipes supply them in sufficient amounts. For more on this, read Chapter V on supplements.

There are standards set by the federal government for the daily minimum requirements of these elements. While I would never want to upset the balance by emphasizing one or other nutrient, I do believe that minimum requirements are just that, minimal, and that there must also be optimum or best levels of nutrients in a diet.

15

You will find some of the recipes have the percentages of proteins, fats and carbohydrates given. These figures do not include water content, and so would only be correct if the food were dried or dehydrated. For example, the labels on canned food which give the water content have much lower percentages of nutrients simply because most of the volume is water.

These recipes almost always contain grains and beans in a combination that will increase the usable protein of both. Frances Moore Lappé in her remarkable book, *Diet for a Small Planet* tells why this happens and how to use this combination to advantage. Following her methods, I have calculated how much the percentage of usable protein has increased in a few of the recipes because of this happy union of grains, legumes and seeds. This protein increase is not to be added to the percentage of protein given in the recipe, but as no protein is 100% usable by the body, it means that the amount absorbed during digestion is increased by the percentage given. Read her book for further information.

Remember when you use vegetarian recipes for your cat, they must be supplemented with extra protein in the form of meat, eggs, fish, or poultry.

Most of these recipes are edible and nourishing for people.

Some Helpful Figures and Proportions On How Much to Feed

1) Not more than one fourth of a dog's diet should be meat or fish.

2) A dog that is kept outside during winter should be given up to twice as much food as an indoor dog.

3) An adult dog weighing 20 lbs. should consume about 700 calories a day, a 40 lb. dog, 1160 calories, a 66 lb. dog 1650 calories a day, and a 150 lb. dog, 3600 calories a day.*

4) For each pound a 5 week old puppy weighs, he should eat about 100 calories a day.*

5) A 14 week old dog weighing 20 lbs. can eat 960 calories a day.*

6) Cats need almost twice as much protein as dogs.

7) Cats need more than twice as much B-complex vitamins as dogs. A good source of this is brewers yeast.

8) An adult cat weighing 8 to 12 lbs. normally eats 300 to 400 calories in about 6 ounces of food a day. One third of this should be protein.

9) For each pound a kitten weighs, he should eat about 115 calories a day.

10) For each pound a young cat weighs, he should be getting 70 calories a day. This amounts to 350 calories for a 5 pound cat.

11) Kittens and puppies need twice as much food as older animals.

*"The Collins Guide to Dog Nutrition" by Donald R. Collins, DVM. This book has complete charts on the food requirements of dogs and puppies.

12) Kittens and puppies quadruple their weight in 4 weeks. A nursing mother needs lots of calcium as she can lose one third of her own calcium from her bones by supplying it in her milk. Bone meal is the best supplement for calcium.

13) A cat feeding four kittens can eat a pound of meat a day.

14) Calcium and phosphorus in a cat's or dog's diet should be at a one to one ratio. Since meat has 15 to 30 times as much phosphorus as calcium, bone meal or calcium supplements should be added. A meat meal should contain 5 to 10% calcium measured on a dry basis.

An adult cat needs 400 to 800 mg. of calcium a day (¼ teaspoon bonemeal). A 50 lb. dog needs about 3000 mg. of calcium a day (1½ teaspoons bonemeal).

Don't get too hung up on these figures, they are only guides to help you know where you are.

III RECIPES

SOME WAYS TO CUT COSTS TO THE BONE

Feeding our pets as well and as cheaply as possible becomes more and more important with the prices of everything rising to the point where I fear some of us cannot afford to keep our animal friends any longer. I don't like to think about this possibility, so I have included some very low cost alternatives that seem to me to be good solutions.

First, the use of leftovers is a tradition as old as the relationship between man and beast. Leftovers are so much better fed to your pet the same day you prepare the food rather than being kept, cluttering up the refrigerator to be disguised some way and fed to the family at a later date. This immediate consumption is much healthier too, for all, including pets. There is a very long lived, healthy group of people, living

19

in a remote section of Russia, who give all leftovers to their animals and cook everything
fresh each meal even if the interval is only a matter of hours.

Bones

I give meaty bones, raw or cooked, to my
dogs, while the cats get chicken bones, wing tips
and hind ends, cooked or raw. Our cats seem
clever enough not to choke on such bones.
However many pet owners never give a chicken
bone to their cats, so I won't recommend them,
or fish or pork bones either, which can splinter.

Marrow Bones

These are the greatest. I just bake them in a
moderate oven for twenty (20) minutes to one
half hour, let them cool, and scoop out the marrow. (You can try the marrow on toast yourself.
It's delicious and strengthening.) Give your dog
the rest of the marrow with cereal or cooked
vegetables, or give him a bone with the marrow
in it. The rest of the bones can be used in the next
recipe.

Mother Hubbard's Soup Bone Stock

Beg or buy bones from your butcher, or use
bones left over from roasts, or turkey and chicken
carcasses. Add any meat trimming and scraps
you can find. Cover with water, add about one
tablespoon of sea salt, and two tablespoons of
vinegar. Cover and simmer for three to four
hours or longer. The vinegar and salt help ex-
tract the valuable minerals from the bones. Fido

may have to share the stock if you want some of the soup yourself. Give him whatever bones seem alright to gnaw on. The poultry bones may be soft enough to crumble over his other foods and any leftover stock can be used in the next recipe, or poured over your pet's dry food. I find a milk carton handy for storing this nourishing liquid.

Kitty and Doggy Pot au Feu

This recipe is from my friends Nance Mc-Crohon and Mary Brekke in Crete, Illinois. They average three to five dogs apiece due to their kind hearts, tolerant husbands, and the frequency of lost or dumped animals in their neighborhood.

Keep a pot of liquid simmering slowly on the back burner or your stove consisting of stock or water and one or two boullion cubes. Add to it all leftovers from the day, except of course, sweet things or desserts. You can throw in left-over non-sugared cereals, sandwich leavings, pizza, meats, salads, bones, vegetables, gravies, carrots, potato skins, pea pods, parsley, outer leaves of lettuce, celery, cabbage, stalks of vegetables you don't use such as broccoli, collards, spinach, asparagus—in short, anything that is still edible. You'd be surprised how nourishing leftover peanut butter or vegetable leaves are used this way. Remember, especially if you are a mother of children who won't finish anything, how lucky you are to have a pet who will. So you don't have to throw food out and feel guilty or worse yet, eat it yourself and gain weight.

Cook your *Pot au Feu* slowly, not more than

an hour. Give your pet whatever solids he likes along with the liquid. This can be poured over dry food or cereal which has been fortified with ½ teaspoon of brewers yeast, ¼ teaspoon bone meal, and 2-3 drops of cod liver oil per cat or ½ tablespoon yeast, 1 teaspoon bone meal, and ½ teaspoon cod liver oil per middle-sized dog. Whatever you don't use can be stored.

Shopping Day Stock

When you come home with your groceries and are about to put them away, get out a pot and as you wash and trim your vegetable and salad greens, put the discarded but edible pieces in the pot. If you have a blender, chop them in water first. Add chicken necks, gizzards and any other meat scraps you have. Simmer for 15 minutes to one hour depending on how fine the vegetables are chopped. While your concoction is simmering you can throw in some oats or wheat cereal, if you like to thicken it, and add some soy flour for extra protein. I store this stock in a milk carton and use it over dry food, meat or cereal, fortified with yeast, cod liver oil and bone-meal as in the recipe for Pot au Feu above.

Fishhead Stew or Mehitabel's Bouillabaise

This time, buy or beg from a fish market or the fish counter of your supermarket, some fish-heads—preferably big ones—fishtails and other scraps. Place in a large pot with some chopped carrots, celery tops, perhaps a few feathery car-rot tops, onions, green pepper cores and a few seeds. The vegetables can be chopped in a blender. Add water to cover, and simmer for about 15 to 20 minutes. Remove the bones from the fish and serve over converted or brown rice, cereal or potatoes, fortified with yeast, cod liver oil and bonemeal as in the recipe for Pot au Feu above.

The *Pot au Feu, Shopping Day Stock,* and *Bouillibaise* above can be made into complete meals by slowly adding to the boiling liquid one or two cups of brown or converted rice, corn meal, barley, oats, or cracked wheat, and one cup of any type of dry beans. Do not allow the liquid to stop boiling. This allows the heat to penetrate and thoroughly cook the beans and grain. As soon as everything has been added, turn down the heat and simmer slowly for one or two hours, adding more liquid if necessary.

23

This should make a nutritious food for a dog. A cat may require more protein unless there is enough meat or fish to begin with. To add protein, add a coddled egg, cottage cheese, some raw liver, or some more meat or fish. Don't forget to add the brewers yeast, cod liver oil and bone meal.

Very Cheap Cereal for Dogs —to use when you really are scratching the bottom of the barrel.

This recipe uses "scratch"—a chicken feed made of corn, oats and barley, which can be bought at a feed store for a few cents a pound. Get the finest grind.

2½ cups water, beef or vegetable stock
4 tablespoons powdered milk
1 teaspoon salt (sea for minerals)
1 cup chicken scratch
¼ cup soy grits or soy beans, soaked
    overnight and pulverized in a blender

Bring water or stock to boiling point. Add rest of ingredients. Bring to boil and simmer for 30 minutes until liquid is absorbed. Cool and add:

1½ tablespoons corn oil or fat
2 tablespoons brewers yeast
¼ teaspoon cod liver oil
1 tablespoon alfalfa meal
1 teaspoon bone meal

Use as is or along with dry cereal food and serve with meat if you have some, and vegetables.

I use this recipe for my dogs since cats may not like the grainy feeling of the corn.

Protein 24%   Fat 19%   Carbohydrate 57%
Calories 800

Because the proteins are complementary, the usable protein is increased by 13%. See pg. 16.

My daughter and son-in-law, Debbie and Michael Rouse discovered "scratch" while living frugally on a farm with their chickens. They fed it to their two dogs along with their leftovers every day, but they warn that as a steady diet, this cereal needs supplements. If they seem to need it, give some extra vitamins and minerals once in a while.

Very Cheap Cereal with Meat for Dogs

This is the same as the previous recipe, but add to the pot one lb. of liver scraps, meat scraps or any combination of meat, liver, kidney, heart, lung or tripe. Some stores package this kind of thing and sell it cheaply as pet food. Cut the meat into manageable pieces and simmer 1 to 5 minutes longer.

Chicken Loaf

> 2 lbs. chicken necks—ground. Ask your butcher to grind them or put them (partly frozen is easiest) through a meat chopper. The easiest way is to take a heavy utensil such as a rolling pin or a tenderizer and smash them flat, then chop them up with a sharp knife.
> 1 cup fresh greens—broccoli, celery, collards, outer romaine leaves, spinach or any other greens you happen to have. Chop them in a blender with some water or stock.
> 1 clove garlic—chop with greens above
> 2 tablespoons bacon fat
> 2 slices grated whole wheat bread
> 1 egg

Mix all together in a bowl, then place in used dog or cat food cans if you have them, or any other containers suitable for baking. Bake 30 to 45 minutes or until firm and slightly brown.

Doggie Crunchies

> 1 cup chicken scratch
> ½ cup soy flour or ¼ cup soy grits or raw whole beans
> ½ teaspoon sea salt or 1 tablespoon kelp, powdered
> 2 tablespoons buckwheat* flour, groats, or pancake mix
> 2 tablespoons cotton seed oil, or any other oil
> A few drops wheat germ oil to retard rancidity.
> 1 egg
> ½ teaspoon bone meal

Soak the scratch and the whole soy beans if you are using them, for a few hours or overnight. Drain off part of the water, retaining just enough to grind it in a blender until smooth. Add the remaining ingredients and mix. Spread on an oiled cookie sheet and bake 30 minutes at 350 degrees, or until toasted (but not browned). Break into pieces and serve. If it is too soft, dry it in the oven with the heat turned off.

*I use buckwheat because it is very nutritious as well as being a relatively inexpensive whole grain.

Protein 19%   Fat 25%   Carbohydrate 56%

Because the proteins are complementary the usable protein is increased by 13%, see pg. 16.

How To Turn Your Daily Leftovers Into Pet Food

After your meal is over, collect the leftovers from the plates. Let us say that your meal consisted of meat or fish, potatoes or noodles, a cooked vegetable, and a tossed salad. Perhaps a bit of bread and butter is included and some milk. Discard the bread if it is white and most of the noodles, as white flour will do your pet very little good at all, but a few noodles will add palatability. Most desserts are unsuitable as are sweet gelatin salad molds. Some people, in—cluding me, allow their pets the pleasure of licking up the extra ice cream from the plates, but that is up to you.

Now back to the kitchen. Put your leftover salad (dressing is fine, don't pour it off) in a blender with enough water to mince the vegetables, or chop them yourself with a knife. Pour these into the empty roasting pan or the pot the meat or fish was cooked in. Bring it to a boil and stir to take up the cooked on meat juices and fat.* Now put your left-over vegetables and liquids they were cooked in into the blender, mince them and add to the pot or pan. Do include baked potato skins and whole wheat bread crusts which can also be chopped up and added. Now add the meat scraps and plate scrapings. The left over fat can be cut up or can be ground up in the blender with the vegetables.

How you use this mixture depends on its ingredients. If it is about one-fourth meat or fish along with some vegetable starch and fat, serve it to your cat or dog as is. If the fat content is more than half, use it to pour over dry food, or

*If you have made gravy in the pan, just start from there and add the chopped up salad and left-over vegetables to the left-over gravy.

use it with extra meat and dry food. If you have mostly vegetables, add it to their regular meals for its nutritional value. Most cats will refuse more than one teaspoon of any vegetable added to their meals. Dogs will eat at least one or two tablespoons. Try that proportion at first. If they like it, add more.

If you have one cat or a small dog and you have too many leftover vegetables to keep, one good way to preserve them is to pour them into ice cube trays, or you can use narrow plastic bags and fill them like little sausages, twisting each portion separately, and wrapping with a wire tie.

When you are ready to use it, cut off a section and thaw it in a saucepan. Add the rest of the meal to the saucepan and warm it, too. As dogs and cats live by their noses, a warm meal that smells good is much nicer than icebox cold meals.

DRY FOODS AND CEREALS

Kitty or Doggie Crunchies I   —a complete dry food.

> *1 lb. chicken necks and gizzards, ground*
> *(If your butcher won't do this, put it thru a meat grinder).*

28

1 can mackerel, chopped
½ lb. or 2 cups soybean flour, not defatted
1 cup wheat germ
1 cup powdered skim milk
1 cup cornmeal
1 cup rye flour
½ lb. or 2 cups whole wheat flour
3 tablespoons bonemeal
1 tablespoon sea salt, iodized or 3 table-
    spoons kelp, powdered
4 tablespoons oil or fat
1 tablespoon cod liver oil
¼ cups alfalfa powder
3 cloves garlic, minced
½ cup chopped onion (optional)
1 quart water
100 mg. iron supplement
½ cup brewers yeast

Mix ingredients to make firm dough. Spread flat on cookie sheet about ¼ to ½ inch thick. Bake in moderate oven until golden brown, ½ to ¾ hour. Cool, and break into bite size chunks. Sprinkle with ½ C. brewers yeast and place in airtight containers. It will keep a few days without refrigeration. After that place in refrigerator or freezer.

If this is not tempting enough to your pet, try pouring a little bacon fat over it, or some leftover gravy. There are some companies now manufacturing artificial flavors.* Perhaps we soon will be able to purchase yummy flavors to make our good food more irresistible.

Protein 35%   Fat 22%   Carbohydrate 43%

Because soy protein and the proteins in the flours are complimentary, the usable protein in this recipe is increased about 15%. See page 16.

*International Flavors & Fragrances
521 W. 57th Street—New York, New York   29

Doggie and Kitty Crunchies II

This is a vegetarian meal except for bonemeal, and as complete a food as I've been able to put together without meat.

1 cup soybeans or grits—or put soaked whole
   soybeans thru the blender, with 2 cups water
   (See soybean recipes.)
½ cup wheat germ
¾ cup skim milk powder
2 cups whole grain cereal—oatmeal, millet,
   wheat, barley or corn or any mixture.
1 cup bran
½ cup polyunsaturated oil—corn, cottonseed,
   part bacon fat or lard may be used, mixed
   with 1 teaspoon cod liver oil
3 teaspoons bonemeal
½ cup brewers yeast
400 I. units Vitamin E
2 tablespoons kelp powder
1 tablespoon sea salt
2 tablespoons alfalfa powder
50 mg. Iron supplement

Cook cereal, salt and soybean grits together in 2 qts. boiling water as in recipe for 5 Grain Cereal,* for 15 minutes. Add more water if too dry. Cool slightly. Add all remaining ingredients, stirring rapidly. Mix thoroughly and spread rather thin on cookie sheet. Dry in oven at 150 to 200 degrees, until crisp. Break into pieces and serve.

For this or any other cereal recipe, unground wheat which is much cheaper may be used. You can crack the wheat in a blender and increase cooking time to one hour or simmer the unground wheat 3 to 4 hours. You can buy unground wheat at an animal feed store.

*Page 35.

Protein 25%   Fat 25%   Carbohydrate 50%

Because the proteins in the grains and soy are complimentary, the usable protein is increased by 24%. See page 16.

Doggie and Kitty Crunchies III
(Low Calorie)

> ½ cup rice bran or wheat bran
> ¼ cup wheat germ
> 1 cup rye flour
> ½ cup beef flavored soy granules, granburgers, or ¼ cup defatted soy flour
> 1 tablespoon beef drippings, bacon fat or chicken fat or oil
> ½ cup water plus 1 or 2 bouillon cubes
> 1 teaspoon dried parsley or other herb
> 2 whole eggs
> 1 teaspoon bone meal
> 1 tablespoon kelp

Mix, knead, and spread on cookie sheet and bake at 350° until golden and crisp. Break into bite size pieces for dogs. For cats, cut into ribbons or very small squares before it is baked.

This is not a complete meal type of crunchies but is a palatable high protein biscuit with a meat flavor.

Protein 23% Fat 19% Carbohydrate 58%

Cereals

Wheat is the most convenient and widely used of all grains. It is also the most abused during the manufacturing process it must undergo before it becomes generally available as food. When using wheat or any other food in these recipes I try to get back to the original article. Wheat can be bought whole (called wheat berries) cracked, flaked, ground into a meal, or finely ground into a flour. Most of these products can be got in health food stores and some of them very cheaply at a feed store. All of these can be made into cereals. Adding ⅛ cup of soy grits or ¼ cup of soy flour per cup of wheat increases the usable protein by 32%. See page 16.

Whole Wheat Cereal

> 1 cup cracked or flaked wheat
> ⅛ cup soy grits or ¼ cup soy flour
> 2 cups water
> ½ teaspoon bone meal
> 1 teaspoon kelp

Add wheat and soy slowly to boiling water and simmer covered for 15 minutes or until done. Wheat germ or wheat germ and middlings can be substituted for wheat.

Whole Wheat Mush

> 1 cup whole wheat flour
> ¼ cup soy flour
> 3 cups water
> ½ teaspoon bone meal
> 1 teaspoon kelp

Toast the flours first for a better flavor. Spread them on a cookie sheet and put in the oven at 350° shaking every so often until lightly toasted. Then add one cup of the flour to three cups of boiling water, stirring all the while. Simmer for about ½ hour or until done. If you cook it in a double boiler it will take about one hour.

If you don't have whole grain flour or cereal or want to use up some white flour, add ¼ cup of bran and 2 tablespoons of wheat germ to ¾ cup flour for each cup of whole wheat flour. Your dogs and cats do not mind meal worms if you have buggy cereals or grains. They will finish it for you if you cook it for them. The best bran and wheat germ are found in bulk in most health food stores and are surprisingly cheap. Keep wheat germ in the refrigerator.

Unground Wheat Cereal

Slowly add one cup wheat berries to 3½ cups rapidly boiling water, meat or vegetable stock. Season with 1 tablespoon kelp. Simmer covered for 4 hours. Add ¼ cup bacon fat and 1 teaspoon garlic powder. Serve it plain or over cooked corn, cabbage, or carrots and an equal amount of beef or pork liver. The liver can be used raw or added during the last few minutes of cooking.

Cornmeal

Cornmeal is a very inexpensive food to buy, and like wheat and other grains, combines with soy flour or beans to make a good high protein for a dog or cat. Cornmeal is made from dried field corn which is also fed to cattle. If you really want to save money, go to a feed store and buy the dried corn on the cobs or as kernels and grind your own in a blender or food chopper, or do it like the Indians did with a large mortar and pestle. Once you have it ground, use it up at once or keep it in the refrigerator for it is not de-germinated as the store-bought cornmeal is.

Corn Meal Mush

Place 1 cup of cornmeal in one cup of water to wet it. Boil another cup of water, add the corn and water mixture and cook it slowly for about 15 to 20 minutes, stirring once in awhile, until it is thickened. If you add ¼ cup of soy flour to the cornmeal you can increase the usable protein content up to 50%. See page 16.

Before it cools completely, pour the left-over cornmeal into a pan and refrigerate it. It can then be sliced and fried, or just sliced and buttered, or served with milk.

Millet, Buckwheat, Rice, Oats, and Barley

These are excellent cereals for your pet. In some ways they are superior to wheat as they are easier to digest and contain different but just as valuable trace minerals. If your pet is over-weight or is constipated or if he is suffering from diarrhea, it may be because he cannot tolerate wheat, so in that case use corn and these other grains instead. However, wheat germ and wheat bran are such great foods, they probably still can and should be used.

Prepare these grains the same as the wheat cereal above, but use ½ to one more cup of boiling water for the buckwheat, rice and millet, and if you are using brown rice, cook it for 40 minutes.

34

Three Grain Cereal

  ½ cup rolled oats
  ½ cup buckwheat groats (kasha)
  ½ cup millet
  ¼ cup soy grits or flour
  2 tablespoons kelp
  ¼ cup bacon fat or oil
  ½ tablespoon bonemeal
  ¼ cup brewers yeast
  ½ teaspoon cod liver oil

Boil 4 cups water. Mix dry ingredients to prevent lumping and stir them slowly into the boiling water. Don't let the boiling stop. This opens the starch granules so they are more easily digested.* Cover and simmer for 15 or 20 minutes. Add the bone meal, yeast and cod liver oil. If you are using the supplements in chapter V, the last three ingredients are not necessary.

Five Grain Cereal

  ½ cup cracked wheat
  ½ cup corn meal
  ½ cup rolled oats
  2 teaspoons salt (sea) or 3 tablespoons kelp
    (powdered)
  ¼ cup buckwheat groats (Kasha)
  ¼ cup soybean meal or grits
  ¼ cup millet
  ¼ cup oil or fat
  1 tablespoon bone meal
  ½ cup brewers yeast
  1 teaspoon cod liver oil

Boil 6 cups water. Add salt. Mix all the dry cereals together to prevent lumping. Stir slowly into boiling water. Don't let the boiling stop.

*Dogs and cats do not begin the digestive process of starch in the mouth as we do.

35

This opens the starch granules so they are more easily digested. Add oil or fat. (Unsaturated oil is healthiest.) Cover and simmer for 30 minutes. Add bonemeal, kelp, yeast and cod liver oil, if you are not using the supplements in chapter V.

Kasha

This is made of buckwheat groats which rate quite high in nutrition and are low in cost. When I made this it was so delicious we ate most of it ourselves.

>   1 cup buckwheat groats
>   1 egg
>   1 small onion, chopped
>   2 tablespoons chicken fat or shortening
>   2 cups of boiling water with two chicken
>   bouillon cubes

Mix beaten egg and groats together and put them in a dry skillet. Heat and stir with a spatula until each grain is light and separate. Saute the onions in chicken fat. Add them to the groats along with the boiling stock which you add gradually. Cover the skillet or pan and cook slowly on top of the stove until the liquid if absorbed. This can also be baked covered for 30 minutes at 350°.

Scrapple

Scrapple is like the name sounds. You use up your scraps.

> 6 cups of meat broth
> 2 cups cornmeal or rolled oats or any
>   combination
> ½ cup wheat germ
> ½ cup soy flour
> 2 or more cups meat or poultry scraps
>   with fat
> 1 cup of tomatos or tomato sauce
> 1 cup leftover vegetables
>   minced onion or garlic
> 1 teaspoon sage or marjoram
> 1 teaspoon bone meal
> 2 tablespoons of kelp or 2 teaspoons of
>   sea salt
> ¼ teaspoon cayenne pepper

Mix the cornmeal with some of the cold broth to wet it. This is not necessary with other grains. Boil the remaining broth and add the oats, soy flour, cornmeal, and wheat germ mixed together to prevent lumping. Cook in a double boiler until thick. Add the vegetables, meat scraps, seasonings and bone meal and cook a bit longer. Pour into wet loaf pans and let set overnight. The next day slice it and serve it as is or fry it like mush.

When supplemented (see chapter V) this makes a very good all-round food for a dog.

37

DOGGY WANT A CRACKER?

Rye Crisps

> 1 cup rye flour
> ¼ cup soy bean flour
> 3 tablespoons lard, bacon fat or oil mixed with
> ⅓ cup water
> ½ teaspoon bone meal

Mix flours. Add liquid. Mix well. Roll out on cookie sheet and bake until golden brown at 350 degrees.

Wheat Crisps

> 1 cup whole wheat flour
> ¼ cup soy bean flour
> 3 tablespoons lard, bacon fat or oil, mixed with
> ⅓ cup water
> ½ teaspoon bone meal

Mix and bake as for Rye Crisps.

Oatmeal Crisps

> ½ cup whole wheat flour
> ¼ cup soy bean flour
> 1 cup rolled oats
> 4 tablespoons lard, bacon fat or oil, mixed with
> ½ cup water
> ½ teaspoon bone meal

Mix and bake at for Rye Crisps.

Vitamin Crisps

> 1 cup whole wheat flour
> ½ cup cooked greens, chopped in a blender (spinach, kale, turnip greens, swiss chard, etc.)
> 2 tablespoons oil or bacon fat
> 1 tablespoon alfalfa meal
> 2 tablespoons brewers yeast
> ¾ teaspoon bone meal

Mix ingredients together. Add enough milk, stock or water to make a firm dough. Roll out flat on a cookie sheet. Bake at 350 degrees until barely brown.

(½ cup chopped, cooked carrots may be used instead of greens)

All these crackers contain about 16% protein, 25% fat, 59% carbohydrate. However the usable protein is increased by 30% because of the complimentary combination of wheat and soy. See page 16.

Hard Biscuits for Dogs and Cats

> 1 cup whole wheat flour
> 2 tablespoons wheat germ
> ¼ cup bran flakes
> ¼ cup soy flour
> 1 tablespoon molasses (unsulphered)
> 2 tablespoons oil or fat
> 1 tablespoon kelp or 1 teaspoon salt
> 1 teaspoon sage
> ½ teaspoon bone meal
> ⅓ cup milk or water

Mix all ingredients together. Knead and shape into crescents, rounds or sticks for dogs. For cats, roll out and cut into narrow strips or ribbons. Bake 25-30 minutes in a moderate oven (350°) until lightly toasted. Watch the narrow strips as they tend to get done sooner than the others. If the biscuits are not hard enough, leave them in the oven with the heat turned off for an hour or as long as desired.

15% Protein   21% Fat   64% Carbohydrate

The soy and wheat combination increases the usable protein by 26%. See page 16.

Dog Biscuits De Luxe

> 2 cups whole wheat flour
> ¼ cup corn meal
> ½ cup soy flour
> ½ cup sunflower seeds or pumpkin seeds
> 1 teaspoon salt
> 2 eggs mixed with ¼ cup milk
> 2 tablespoons butter, fat, or oil
> ¼ cup unsulphered molasses
> 1 teaspoon bone meal

Mix dry ingredients and seeds together. Add melted shortening of oil, honey and egg mixture, except for one tablespoon. Add more milk if needed to make a firm dough. Knead together for a few minutes and let the dough rest for ½ hour or more. Roll out to ½ inch. Cut into shapes and brush with the remainder of the egg milk mixture. Bake in moderate oven (350°) for 30 minutes or until lightly toasted. To make a harder biscuit, leave them in the oven with the heat turned off for an hour or more.

Biscuits keep longer if you use corn oil instead of butter.

18% Protein   19% Fat   63% Carbohydrates

The soy, seeds and flours combine to increase the usable protein by 42%. See page 16.

Kitty Catnip Cookies

> 1 cup whole wheat flour
> 2 tablespoons wheat germ
> ¼ cup soy flour
> ⅓ cup powdered milk
> 1 tablespoon kelp
> ½ teaspoon bone meal
> 1 teaspoon crushed dried catnip leaves
> 1 tablespoon unsulphered molasses

1 egg
2 tablespoons oil, butter or fat
⅓ cup milk or water

Mix dry ingredients together. Add the molasses, egg, oil, and milk or water. Roll out flat on an oiled cookie sheet and cut into narrow strips or ribbons. Bake 20 minutes in a moderate (350°) oven until lightly toasted. Break into pea sized pieces as cats usually do not like big hunks.

Protein 20%   Fat 18%   Carbohydrate 62%

Cat and Dog Cakes or Petah

2 cups whole wheat flour
½ cup soy flour
1 cup milk, water, or stock
1 tablespoon honey or molasses
1 teaspoon corn oil
1 teaspoon salt
1 teaspoon bonemeal

Mix dry ingredients, add the liquid and the honey or molasses. Mix and let the dough rest in a warm place for 15 minutes to ½ hour. Add the oil and allow to sit another half hour. Take walnut size portions of dough and flatten into cakes. Bake quickly on a hot skillet until lightly browned.

This dough may be also made into flat cakes and baked in an oven at 400° for one half hour. For cats, roll dough to ¼ inch and bake on a sheet scored into small sections ¼ inch square or smaller, as cats do not usually like big lumps.

Carob Cakes

    1 cup whole wheat flour
    ¼ cup soy flour
    ¼ cup carob
    1 egg mixed with ¼ cup milk
    1 tablespoon honey
    2 teaspoon kelp or 1 teaspoon salt
    2 tablespoons oil or fat
    ½ teaspoon bone meal

Mix, knead, roll out or make walnut size balls with your hands and flatten out on an oiled cookie sheet. Bake about 30 minutes at 350° as in recipe for Hard Biscuits for Dogs and Cats.

Carob tastes a little like chocolate, but unlike chocolate, it is very good for critters as well as people as it is amazingly high in calcium. It has four times as much calcium as phosphorous which is quite unusual and it has almost as much fiber content as natural raw bran. Look for it in a health food store. It is not expensive.

Corn Bread

    1 cup cornmeal
    ¼ cup soy flour
    ¼ cup whole wheat flour
    ½ teaspoon bone meal
    1 egg
    1 cup milk or buttermilk

Mix dry ingredients. Add egg and milk and mix well. Bake in an oiled bread pan at 375° for 30 minutes.

Corn Chapatties

>   1 cup cornmeal
>   ¼ cup soy flour
>   1 tablespoon corn oil or fat
>   ¼ cup powdered milk
>   ½ teaspoon bone meal
>   2 cups boiling water

Add the boiling water to the cornmeal, flour, powdered milk and oil and mix well. Take a small lump in your hand and flatten it out quite thin. Bake it slowly on an oiled griddle, turning over to cook each side.

Johnny Cake

Use the same mixture as for corn chapatties above, and spread the whole mixture about ¼ inch thick on a cookie sheet and bake at 350° until done. Sesame seeds or celery seeds can be sprinkled on this cake before baking, for extra taste and nourishment.

Hush Puppies

I couldn't finish the chapter without this one.

>   1 cup cornmeal
>   ¼ cup soy flour
>   1 rounded teaspoon wheat flour
>   ½ teaspoon baking soda
>   ½ teaspoon bone meal
>   ½ cup buttermilk
>   1 egg, beaten
>   ½ onion grated

Mix the dry ingredients together. Add the rest of the ingredients, shape into small balls and fry in deep fat until brown.

43

BEANS AND SOYBEANS

The addition of soybeans to any dish will make it a much more nutritious meal. Dorothea Van Grundy Jones says in her book, *The Soybean Cook Book*, "Soybeans are the best source of protein from the vegetable kingdom and can honestly claim the title 'the meat that grows on vines.'" According to Ms. Jones, soybeans contain more protein than meat, fish or lima beans, up to three times as much protein as eggs or whole wheat flour, and eleven times as much as milk! Not only that, this astounding vegetable is very inexpensive if you can buy it at a farm stand or an animal feed store. It can also be found in health food stores and some groceries as flour, powder, granules, grits, and whole beans. It is probably still a good buy wherever and however you find it.

Soy flour is made from ground raw soybeans. It is also made from beans after the oil has been extracted. This is called defatted soy flour. This kind of soy flour has over 52% protein. Either one can be used in these recipes.

Soy or soya powder is usually a lightly toasted flour and it is sweeter and nuttier in flavor.

Soy grits are beans that have been chopped into at least ten pieces. If a crunchy texture is wanted, soy grits can be substituted for soy flour in any recipe. You can make your own soy grits if you have a blender or a food chopper. See recipe below for homemade soy grits.

How To Cook Soybeans

I have been searching for a long time to find the best way to cook soybeans. The usual way it to soak the beans overnight, then simmer them in a pot for an hour or so. Freezing the soaked beans, chopping them into small pieces, and adding vinegar to the cooking water, all shorten the cooking time considerably. For pets, beans are best served mashed or chopped.

Cooked Whole Soybeans

> 1 cup dry soybeans
> 3 cups water
> 1 tablespoon vinegar

Soak the beans in water for a few hours and place them in a freezer overnight. The next morning place the beans in a pot with 3 cups of fresh water and the vinegar. Bring to a boil over high heat, then turn it down to a simmer and cook gently for 40 minutes to 1 hour. If a soft bean is wanted, these beans must be cooked up to five hours or more.

Soy beans can also be cooked in a pressure cooker with 2 cups of water per cup of beans, at 15 lbs. of pressure for 20 to 30 minutes. Follow the directions that came with your cooker.

Homemade Soy Grits

Crack the dry beans into a meal in your blender, food mill, or meat chopper. Soak them in water for several hours or overnight like the whole beans, drain thoroughly through a fine strainer, and spread the chopped beans on a cookie sheet to dry. Place in an oven at 200° for an hour or so shaking once in a while until the grits are lightly toasted to a light brown color. These can be used in any recipe calling for soy grits or meal.

There is a new book, *The Book of Tofu* by William Shurtleff and Akiko Aoyagi, which has a very good method that makes use of a raw bean puree made from soaked beans. After the beans are soaked overnight, they are combined with fresh water and mashed in a blender or food grinder until smooth. This puree called "gô" can be substituted in most recipes for cooked grits, mashed soybeans or soybean mash, I believe, as long as the recipe calls for further cooking or baking as in the Soy Loaf recipe. It is recommended that the gô be used up at once as it does not keep well.

Soy Grits Cereal

> 1 cup soy grits
> 2 cups water
> ½ teaspoon salt

Add the grits slowly to boiling salted water and cook gently for a few minutes until all the water is absorbed.

Soy Loaf

> 1 cup soy grits cereal or cooked and mashed soy beans
> ½ cup celery, onion, green pepper
> 1 clove garlic
> 1 egg
> 1 teaspoon diced parsley
> ½ cup whole wheat bread crumbs—can be made in a blender
> ½ cup stock, bouillon or liquid from cooked grits

Place egg and liquid in a blender. Add

vegetables and garlic, herbs and seasonings
and blend until chopped fine. Add to grits and
bread crumbs and bake at 350° for ½ hour.

Soy Patties

> 1 cup soy grits cereal or soy bean mash from
>   making soy milk
> 1 egg
> 1 tablespoon chopped onions
> ½ teaspoon sage or rosemary
> ½ teaspoon kelp
> ⅓ cup wheat germ or ½ cup whole wheat
>   bread crumbs

Mix all ingredients and shape into patties.
Cook in oil or bacon fat. Serve with biscuits or
whole wheat bread.

Soy Bean Milk

This is an excellent and healthful substitute
for milk if your pet cannot tolerate milk, and a
great food in any case. Here are three ways of
making it, two using soy beans and one using
flour.

I   1 cup dry soy beans
        3 cups water
        1 tablespoon vinegar
        honey or malt to taste

Soak beans in water for several hours and
place in a freezer overnight. Next morning place
beans in a kettle with fresh water, 3 cups to each
cup of beans and the vinegar. Bring to a boil and
simmer for 40 minutes or longer. Cool slightly
and liquify in a blender. If you are using a food
chopper, drain the beans and put through a fine
blade, then recombine with the cooking water.

Mix well and use as is, or strain through a fine sieve or cheese cloth. Add honey or malt to taste. The solids or mash can be added to other dishes such as meat loaves, cereals, soups, soy patties or soy bean loaf above.

II   Using the gô method (see page 46) liquefy each cup of soaked beans with three cups of fresh water (no vinegar) for 15 minutes in a large stainless steel or porcelain pot. Do not use aluminum.

III   *1 cup soy flour or powder*
3 cups water
malt or honey to taste

Mix well—a blender or a mixer is helpful—and let stand two hours. Boil for 25 minutes in a flat bottomed pan stirring with a spatula. It can also be cooked in a double boiler for 40 minutes. Add malt or honey when cooled. I have never enjoyed the taste of soybean milk made this way, and use it mainly in recipes as called for.

Other Beans, Peas and Lentils.

The larger, harder-to-cook beans can be soaked overnight in cold water, or soaked 2 hours and put in freezer for 2 hours. Using the same water, add salt and bring to a boil and cook for 1-2 hours until done. Vinegar can also be added to the cooking water for quicker cooking.

Beans can also be added to boiling water, simmered for 5 minutes, then cover and let sit for two hours. Bring to a boil and cook as above.

Most beans, peas and lentils need not be

soaked at all if they are added slowly to boiling water so that the boiling does not stop. Then be sure to lower heat immediately and simmer until done. Add 1 teaspoon salt and 2 teaspoons vinegar to each quart of cooking water.

These and perhaps soybeans too, are called pulses. They are what some very strong and heroic figures in the Bible lived on, refusing all meats and fancy gourmet dishes. Perhaps if Daniel were a meat eater or the lions ate pulses, that story might have turned out differently.

Bean Burgers

Dried corn and beans are still economy foods, and mixed together make a nourishing complete protein meal. Use enough bacon fat in the skillet to make the burgers taste good to your pet.

> 1 cup cooked mashed pinto, navy or
>   other beans
> 2 tablespoons corn meal
> 1 heaping teaspoon of flour
> pinch of salt
> bean water
> bacon fat

Mix the first four ingredients with enough bean water to hold together. Drop by tablespoonfuls on a hot skillet greased with bacon fat. Press down with a spatula. Brown on both sides and serve.

Lentil Stew with Rice

Dried lentils are probably the cheapest source of protein available in a grocery store costing today under 10¢ a serving. Combined with a cereal or grain, lentils make a complete protein and a very satisfactory meal. Pea beans, chickpeas, navy beans or any other legume may also be substituted along with any other grain such as barley, wheat or millet.

> ½ cup dried lentils
> 1⅓ cups brown or converted rice
> 2 cups water
> 2 cups canned tomatoes
> 1 tablespoon kelp
> 1 clove garlic
> 1 carrot, chopped
> 3 tablespoons oil or bacon fat or chunk of salt pork or bacon
> 1 teaspoon bone meal

Slowly add all ingredients to boiling water and simmer for ½ to 1 hour.

Protein 13%   Fat 13%   Carbohydrate 74%

The combination of proteins in the rice and beans increases the value of usable protein by 43%. See page 16.

Lentil Loaf

> 1 cup lentils
> 2 cups rolled oats or cornmeal
> ¼ cup soy meal or flour
> 3 cups water or stock
> 1 tablespoon kelp
> 1 or 2 eggs, lightly beaten
> 1 small onion, chopped
> 1 clove garlic
> ¼ cup oil or bacon fat
> 1 teaspoon bone meal

Slowly add lentils to boiling water and simmer for 20 minutes. Add oats or cornmeal and soy grits. Allow to soak for 10 minutes in hot liquid. Add rest of the ingredients, mix well and put in loaf pan. Bake for ½ hour at 350 degrees.

Protein 22%   Fat 18%   Carbohydrate 60%

MILK AND EGGS

Milk in all its forms is an excellent food. However, not all animals or people are able to digest fresh whole milk properly and they get diarrhea or the scours as it is sometimes called in animals. This is usually due to an inability to digest the lactose or milk sugar in the intestines, converting it to lactic acid. In this case buttermilk, yogurt, cottage cheese, white cheese or soy milk are fine substitutes, and in some cases are less expensive than fresh milk. *Natural Rearing** feeds only raw unpasturized milk to puppies, and if you are a breeder, suggests you keep goats. This is because many vitamins and healing properties in milk are lost in heating or boiling. *Natural Rearing** also uses buttermilk for its worm-removing properties.

*A method of rearing animals according to the laws of nature conceived by Juliette de Bairacli Levy, see *The Complete Herbal Book for the Dog.*

Easy Yogurt

Adapted from a recipe given to me by my friend Aida Born in Florida. She calls it yummy yogurt and it is!

Heat oven to 275°. Put in pot or bowl, milk, evaporated milk, powdered milk, and hot water in any proportion you have or like. I like it fairly thick so I use approximately equal proportions of each. The mixture should be slightly above lukewarm. Stir in 2 tablespoons plain yogurt from the store or from the last batch, and mix thoroughly. Cover and put in the oven. Turn heat *off* immediately and let it stay undisturbed in the oven 8-12 hours, or until thickened.

Add this delicious nourishing food to any dish, or serve it plain.

Yogurt Youthtail

½ to 1 cup yogurt
1 tablespoon brewers yeast
1 tablespoon bran
1 tablespoon wheat germ
1 tablespoon lecithin
1 tablespoon honey
1 teaspoon corn oil

Buttermilk can be used instead of yogurt. Mixed together this should make any old critter feel like a young pup or kitten again.

Buttermilk

Buttermilk is less expensive than milk. You may find it dried or powdered in some grocery stores. Dried buttermilk is the real by-product from churning butter, while the kind you find in cartons is a cultured milk like yogurt. Buttermilk is more easily digested than milk and can be substituted for it in almost any recipe or dish. It is very good in gravies and soups.

Buttermilk Breakfast

> Shredded wheat, rye crisp, buttered toast or any biscuit cereal, or cracker recipe from Chapter 4.
> ½ cup buttermilk
> 1 teaspoon honey

Add 1 teaspoon to 1 tablespoon corn oil depending on the size of your pet. Put broken up biscuits or toast in a bowl. Add honey and pour buttermilk over top.

Buttermilk Stew

> 1 leftover potato cooked and chopped
>   with skin, plus a little butter or oil
> 1 cup buttermilk
> 1 hardboiled egg chopped
> 1 tablespoon brewers yeast
> 1 teaspoon dried parsley or other herb

Mix ingredients in a pan and heat to serving temperature (blood heat or 100° F.) Any kind of meat or fish can be added.

Cheese

Adding cheese to any food will add protein and calcium, both of which are valuable additions for pets. Don't throw away any cheese that is getting hard or moldy. Cut off the moldy edges, grate, slice, or chop it in a blender and add it to any dish or recipe. It can be stored in a freezer to keep it from getting moldy again.

Eggs

Eggs are a nearly perfect form of nourishment. Get in the habit of giving your pets at least two of them a week. Dogs will generally eat eggs any style as long as they are mixed in with their daily foods. With cats you must be clever. If they drink milk, slip an egg nog to them, using yolks only.* Save the whites in your freezer and make an angel food cake for yourself. If you use a blender for the egg nog, drop in part of the shell for extra calcium.

Egg Drop Soup

An easy way to add eggs to any dry food.

Boil ½ to 1 cup water or stock. Stir in 1 egg, slightly beaten. Allow to congeal and serve over meal or biscuits.

(If I drop an egg on the floor, I scoop up as much of the yolk as I can and use as above.)

Bauernfruhstuck —a German dish adapted for pets.

> 1 tablespoon bacon fat
> 1 cooked potato, mashed or chopped,
>   preferably with the skin on
> 1 egg

Heat bacon fat in skillet. Add potato. Heat thoroughly and then add slightly beaten egg. Cook until done, turning over with a spatula.

*Raw egg whites are said to cause a deficiency in biotin, one of the B vitamins and a valuable nutrient.

54

Carrots, parsnips or turnips can be substituted for the potato.

The best way to serve eggs to cats is to mix scrambled eggs with chopped liver or fish.

Scrambled Eggs And Sardines

1 can sardines—use the less expensive,
   larger sardines
1 egg lightly beaten with the oil or liquid
   from the sardine can
1 tablespoon of wheat germ

Grease the pan lightly with oil or butter and heat it. Pour in the egg mixed with wheat germ and sardines. Mix gently as the egg cooks. Cool to warm and serve with dry food or cereal.

Scrambled Eggs And Liver

Dice two slices of liver sausage. Fresh liver can be used also. Lightly beat two eggs. Pour into warmed fat or oil in frying pan. Add the liversausage or diced liver. Mix gently as it cooks. Cool to warm and serve with dry food or cereal.

Salmon Egg Foo Yung

1 egg
¼ cup bran
¼ cup leftover vegetables
¼ cup canned salmon
1 tablespoon chopped celery
1 pinch sea salt or ½ teaspoon kelp
1 tablespoon fat or oil

Add all ingredients to beaten egg. Drop mixture from a large spoon into a heated skillet containing oil or fat. Cook slowly until done. Turn over and cook on other side.

Meatless Lasagna

 1 cup noodles, macaroni or spaghetti plus ½
   cup bran and ¼ cup wheat germ or
 1 cup whole wheat noodles, macaroni or
   spaghetti
 1 cup cottage cheese
 1 or 2 eggs beaten in blender with shells
 1 small can tomato sauce or juice
 1 teaspoon diced herbs—parsley, marjoram,
   basil
 1 clove garlic chopped
 1 small onion chopped
 1 tablespoon oil or fat
 ½ cup leftover cheese, grated

Slowly add noodles to boiling water, cook until done and drain through strainer. Add oil to the pot and saute garlic and onion. Add eggs and tomato sauce and cook slowly stirring well. Then add the cottage cheese and the herbs. Put back the noodles and add the cheese, bran, and wheat germ, mix well and serve.

Welsh "Rabbit"

 1 cup leftover cheese grated
 1 teaspoon butter or oil
 1 egg
 ¼ cup evaporated milk
 ½ teaspoon parsley or herbs
 1 teaspoon kelp

Melt butter in heavy pan over low heat. Add the cheese and stir until melted. Add milk slowly and beaten egg. Blend well and serve on whole wheat or rye toast or crackers.

56

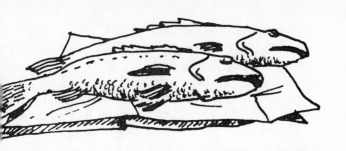

FISH

Fish is a good food for both cats and dogs. I do not think however that cats are as fond of fish as the stories and legends would have it. I don't know many cats who will go near water, much less fish for their dinners, although I once knew an Irish Setter who would walk around in the water near the edge of a lake for hours fishing for minnows.

Too much fish or fish oil is bad for cats as it can give them a painful disease which affects the fat beneath the skin. This is called steatitus or yellow fat disease. So do not give it to your pet every day, and beware of pet foods that put fish in to flavor every variety. Steatitus is caused mainly by rancid fish oil. Vitamin E provides complete protection from this disease, so sprinkle some wheat germ, rice polish, or wheat germ oil over your fish dishes.

It is best to cook most fish for your pets. Steam them gently. The reason is that raw fish has been known to cause a thiamine deficiency (vit. B1) Raw carp and herring will do this but raw perch, catfish and butter fish are probably all right.

Tuna or Mackerel Patties

Combine one can of fish with one or two beaten eggs. Add a minced clove of garlic and some chopped celery and onions if desired, and enough mayonnaise to hold it together. Form into small cakes and gently saute in bacon fat, oil, or butter, or bake in a well oiled pan.

Kitty Potato Fish Dish (Dogs like it too)

This is a good way to use your leftovers, or to cook for your pet along with the family food.

    1 cooked potato
    ½ cup cooked or canned fish (canned mackerel
        is cheap and good)
    2 tablespoons bacon fat or oil
    ¼ cup leftover vegetable, chopped

Combine the potato, fish and vegetable. Add to the melted bacon fat and stir until just warm.

Boiled Squid

Fresh squid must be cleaned as they still have sacs containing bitter fluid. Frozen squid are inexpensive and come cleaned and ready to cook.

With a sharp knife, slice each squid into rings up to the tentacles. Place the rings and tentacles in a pot with 1 cup water, 2 teaspoons vinegar, and a little oil or fat. Boil for 20 minutes. Serve with liquid over dry biscuits or meal.

These rings are delicious French fried. I have served these with cocktails at parties.

Smelts

At certain seasons these can be had for next to nothing a pound. They also are sold frozen in 5 pound boxes and are still inexpensive.

Thaw a few, dip into wheat germ, and saute in oil for a few minutes and serve. If you have a lot to cook at one time, they can be baked in some oil in a moderate oven.

Clam Chowder

> 1 can minced clams
> 1 diced potato—cleaned but not peeled
> 1 tablespoon chopped onion
> 1 tablespoon chopped carrot
> ½ teaspoon kelp
> 2 tablespoons oil or butter
> milk, cream or buttermilk or evaporated milk

Pour clam juice in a pan. Add oil or butter, kelp and vegetables and simmer covered until tender—about 10 to 15 minutes. Add clams, cool and serve over whole wheat toast. Add milk or cream to desired consistency.

The vegetables can be chopped in a blender with the clam juice. If there is not enough liquid, add milk during cooking.

MEAT

I believe that meat for dogs and cats should be cooked as little as possible. Juliette de Baira-cli Levy feeds only raw meat and regards cooked meat and bones as unnatural and unhealthy. She doesn't mind if the meat is a bit gamey, as long as it isn't cooked.

This may sound strange to some, but I remember one day I found some exceedingly smelly uncooked chicken livers in the back of my refrigerator. I decided the only thing to do was to bury them. So all would not be lost, I carefully buried them near the roots of my favorite plants in the front of my house. The next time I looked out, there were my plants, dug up and lying all over the ground, the livers had disappeared and there was Duchess, my Weimeraner dog, with a dirty muzzle and a guilty look. Nothing else happened to her, except for some scolding. Her digestive system was unimpaired. I thought of how many times a dog of ours has brought home a rotten corpse of some unfortunate animal and gleefully rolled around in it. I also remember my friend Nance McCrohon telling us how her dogs love to bury their raw meaty bones and dig them up days or even weeks later when just "right," and chew on them with great relish.

Ms. Levy's *naturally reared* dogs and cats are fed up to 75% raw meat, which includes innards and bones. But unless her methods are strictly followed, not more than one fourth of a dog's diet should consist of meat. Cats should have more meat than dogs, about twice as much. Cooking meat on the stove or in the can destroys the vitamins B1 or thiamine and B6 or pyridoxine. Eating carbohydrates or starches, and especially sugar, increases the need for these very important vitamins so crucial to good health and a well functioning nervous system. That is why I use a lot of brewers yeast and add it after cooking. It is rich in vitamin B1 and will among other things make your pet less hysterical.

Thiamine tablets given along with brewers yeast (non-debittered) have been found to reduce the flea population on a dog or cat, so it may be true that a pet fed only canned or cooked meat lacks thiamine and therefore has fleas. To remedy this, give cats and kittens .5 mg. and dogs .5 to 1 mg. per day extra thiamine along with brewers yeast.

If you use thiamine this way, do *not* overdo it as an oversupply of one B vitamin brings about a deficiency in all the others. Never use it without brewers yeast.

Pyridoxine or vitamin B6 is also destroyed by heat and should be replaced in a diet of cooked meat. Anemia and kidney stones can result from this deficiency. To replace it give cats .3 mg. a day, dogs .5 to 1 mg. a day and puppies 1 mg. a day along with brewers yeast as above.

Always cook pork however, as animals also can get trichinosis.

Beef liver is incredibly high in practically every element needed for well being with the exception of calcium. Beef liver is tops on the nutrition scoreboard* for meat, fish and poultry with a rating of 172 points, followed by chicken breast at 104. Alpo dog food is way down on the list with 30 points and bottom are pure beef hot dogs, 6 points, bacon, 4 points and bologna, 2 points. Remember this the next time you go shopping and compare values and prices. Incidentally, pork liver is just as nutritious as beef liver if not more so.

In his book, *The Collins Guide to Dog Nutrition*, Dr. Collins calls liver "nature's mystery food" because so many dogs have made miraculous recoveries from accidents and illnesses after being given small amounts of raw liver daily—1 teaspoon daily to one tablespoon 3 times a week. What is no mystery he says, is that liver contains more nutrients in one package than any other natural food available to man or beast.

Juliette de Bairacli Levy suggests the answer to this "miracle" may be the folic acid it contains but does not recommend liver more than twice a week.

Raw liver cut in pieces can be fed as is or you can pour boiling water over it, let stand a

*"Nutrition Scoreboard" by Michael Jacobson Ph.D. This is a guide by the Center for Science in the Public Interest that evaluates foods according to several nutritional factors.

few minutes and add to dog food with a tablespoon of corn oil and some bran flakes. For a cat, small dog or puppy use one teaspoon of oil.

Liver And Oatmeal Dish For Cats And Kittens

¼ lb. liver (about one slice)
½ cup dry powdered milk
⅓ cup rolled oats
1 cup boiling water
2 tablespoons oil
1 teaspoon kelp
½ teaspoon bonemeal
1 teaspoon minced parsley

Mix oats and dry powdered milk together and add to one cup of boiling water. Simmer until done, about 10 minutes. Add all the rest of the ingredients including the liver cut into bite size pieces. This is an excellent meal for a cat or kitten. For a dog or puppy, use one half the liver and powdered milk and increase the oatmeal to 1 cup. This will bring the protein down to 29% and the carbohydrate to 49%. This is still pretty high protein for a dog, so it would be good to combine this dish with some cooked potatos or bread.

Protein 35%   Fat 28%   Carbohydrate 37%

63

Beef Heart Meal For Cats And Kittens

Buy a whole beef heart and slice it into steaks or have it ground by your butcher. The steaks are delicious, like very mild liver but meatier.

> ¼ lb. beef heart sliced or ground
> 1 cup potatos, cooked
> 1½ tablespoons oil
> 1 teaspoon brewers yeast
> 1 teaspoon kelp
> ½ teaspoon bonemeal
> 1 teaspoon parsley

Protein 27%   Fat 26%   Carbohydrate 47%

Combine the beef heart with the cooked hot potatos. Add the oil yeast, kelp, bonemeal and parsley, and serve. Like the liver dish above, this is a good high protein meal for felines, but unlike liver which shouldn't be fed to your pet more than twice a week, this beef heart dish can be fed as a regular food. Of course steamed fish or another kind of meat can be substituted for the liver or the heart, and the liver and heart can be used interchangeably.

For a dog's meal use two cups of potatos instead of one. This changes the food values to, Protein 20%   Fat 17%   Carbohydrate 63%

Beef Kidney

Kidneys can be substituted for the heart or liver in the above recipes, or it as well as the heart and liver, can be cut into one inch chunks and served as is. If you would like to cook them, place the chunks in a sauce pan of water to cover and simmer gently for 5 to 10 minutes and serve with the broth poured over cereal, dry food, or vegetables.

Meat Loaf

> 2 tablespoons minced parsley
> 1 lb. hamburger
> 1 lb. ground heart (beef)
> ½ lb. ground beef or pork liver
> 2 eggs, lightly beaten
> 1 tablespoon bonemeal
> ½ cup rolled oats or ½ cup whole wheat
>   bread crumbs
> 1 tablespoon kelp
> 1 teaspoon garlic powder or less
> 1 cup milk, water or tomato juice
> ¼ cup oil or bacon fat

Mix together and bake in a loaf pan for 1 hour at 350 degrees. This loaf is very high in protein and should be served with cereal and vegetables.

Anne's Dog's Dish

My friend Anne Fiacco's dog thrived on this meal. I would add alfalfa meal or a vegetable or two and 1 teaspoon of bone meal.

> ½ lb. ground hamburger meat
> ½ cup brown or converted rice
> ¼ cup corn meal
> 2 cups water or stock

Brown meat in a little oil in a saucepan. Add rice and corn meal and the liquid. Cover and cook 1 hour.

Soy Bean Chili Con Carne

> ½ lb. ground beef
> 1 cup cooked soybeans
> ¼ cup tomato juice or sauce
> 2 tablespoons chopped onions
> 2 tablespoons chopped green pepper
> 1 teaspoon chili powder (optional)
> 2 tablespoons oil or fat

Heat oil in fat in skillet and saute onions and green peppers. Add beef, stir, and cook Slowly a few minutes. Add the rest of the ingredients, cook a few minutes more and serve with converted rice or whole wheat spaghetti with bran flakes sprinkled on top for roughage.

This recipe is a very high protein dish. The chili powder isn't added for atmosphere, but because it is very high in nutrition. Kidney beans or any type of beans can be used.

Lasagna

> ½ lb. ground beef
> 1 #2 can stewed tomatoes
> 1 clove garlic chopped
> 1 small onion chopped
> 1 tablespoon corn oil or fat
> 1 tablespoon dried herbs—parsley, majoram, basil or thyme
> 1 teaspoon kelp
> 1 cup noodles, macaroni or spaghetti plus
> ½ cup bran and ¼ cup wheat germ
> or
> 1 cup whole wheat noodles, macaroni or spaghetti
> ½ cup cottage cheese
> 2 tablespoons brewers yeast and 2 teaspoons bonemeal
> 1 tablespoon honey or unsulphured molasses

Add noodles slowly to a pot of boiling

water and cook until done. Then pour them through a colander or strainer to drain. Add oil to the pot and stir fry the onions, garlic and meat. Add tomatoes, dried herbs and kelp. Simmer for a few minutes and add the cottage cheese, bran and wheat germ if you are using white noodles. Then add the drained noodles, brewers yeast, bonemeal and serve.

The ground beef can be added at the very end if you don't want to cook it.

Tripe

Tripe is good for your pet and if it is a good buy, get some. Cut it into bite size pieces and serve as is. If your dog or cat turns up his nose at it, put it in a pot and make

Triple ala Mode de Canine

½ lb. tripe washed and cut up
2 tablespoons bacon fat
3 tablespoons onions
1 teaspoon rosemary or thyme
1 bay leaf
1 tablespoon parsley
1 tablespoon kelp
2 tablespoons vinegar
¼ cup beans—any kind
1 carrot diced
½ cup celery leaves
1 large unpeeled potato diced
1 small turnip diced
¼ teaspoon cayenne pepper or paprika

Saute tripe in bacon fat in a kettle. Add onions cook a little longer, then add herbs, kelp, vinegar and water to cover, boil and add beans. Simmer covered for 2 hours. Add carrot, celery leaves, turnip and potato. Cook 30 more minutes and serve.

Chicken Neck Stew With Giblets

Collect necks and giblets and store in a freezer. When ready to make stew, thaw them almost completely, place the chicken necks on a firm hard surface and smash them with a rolling pin. With a sharp knife cut the skin and necks into pieces. Also cut up the stomachs and hearts if large enough. Saute the necks and stomachs in oil or fat with some onion. Add some vegetables if desired, cover and let cook for 15 to 20 minutes. Add hearts and livers at the end and serve with rice or potatoes. Fixed this way, chicken necks should be perfectly safe for dogs to eat.

I read somewhere that chicken heads are almost irresistable to cats and very good for them too. If you know where to get some, you could try this. The same source says that if you are feeling squeamish about it, have them wrapped in newspapers, and when you get home, put the package on the floor with your cat and leave the room.

VEGETABLES AND HERBS

Root vegetables such as carrots, potatoes, turnips, beets, parsnips, sweet potatoes and

Jerusalem artichokes*, are all inexpensive vegetables and good for your pet. Just cook some extra along with yours, mash and mix it with his meal. Leave potato skins on as they provide nutrients such as potassium as well as roughage.

Green vegetables such as kale, collards, turnip greens and broccoli are the highest rating vegetables for nutrition in the *Nutrition Scoreboard*** by M. Jacobson. The first three are usually the least expensive vegetables which makes them great buys. My cats are very fond of the first asparagus in spring and I always save the ends for them after I've eaten the tips. This gives them fiber as well as something in asparagus that is very good for kidney and bladder troubles.

Cats are unable to use the vitamin A from greens as dogs and people do, but there are other benefits to be had. Mix one teaspoon of any cooked greens or herbs with a meal for a cat or small dog, unless he likes more. Two tablespoons should do for a medium size dog.

I might mention here that around late winter your pet might start chewing up your house plants. This is not only upsetting to you and your plants, but is also harmful to your cat or dog. Philodendrum, diffenbachia, ivy, azaleas and most spring bulbs are deadly poison and should be kept out of reach, if that is possible with any cat. Feeding green vegetables hopefully might assuage that craving. Also try growing pots of grass seed, oat seeds, catnip or alfalfa.

*Not inexpensive or easy to find, but very easy to grow. If you have enough room to grow sun flowers, you have enough to put in Jerusalem artichokes too.

**A guide that evaluates food by the Center for Science in the Public Interest.

A teaspoon of alfalfa sprouts mixed with kittie's meal would be marvelous for him. If your cat likes his pot of sprouted grass or whatever, try to plant one every week. Just put some potting soil in small pot or dish. Sprinkle seeds over it and cover with a thin layer of soil, water it well and put it in a sunny window. It should be ready in a week. I can't think of any vegetables I wouldn't give to my dogs or cats, but remember always serve them cut small and in small amounts or your pet may refuse to eat the whole meal. Also if you cannot use your vegetable cooking water anywhere else, pour it over your pet's dinner, but not if it is too salty. Taste it first.

Since most vegetables are cooked along with or added to the meals, I do not have many recipes for them, only a few ways to cook them.

Boiled Potatoes, Carrots, Turnips or Other Root Vegetables

Rinse and remove wax from turnips or rutabagas. Cut in pieces and put in saucepan with a small amount of water, a dollup of corn oil or bacon fat and pinch of salt or kelp. Cover and cook gently until soft. Mash with a fork or potato masher, cool and serve.

Leafy Greens Or Herbs

Place a lump of bacon fat in a saucepan, heat and add rinsed and chopped greens with water still clinging to them. Cover tightly and steam over low heat until tender. Cool and serve—2 tablespoons with the meal to a medium sized dog and one teaspoon to a cat. Dandelion greens and nettles cooked this way can also be used.

Peas, Green Beans, Brocolli, Asparagus, Corn Niblets, Cabbage, Cauliflower, Etc.

Boil ½ cup of water, add a pinch of salt or kelp or both, and a lump of fat or spoonful of oil. Add vegetables cut into small pieces, cover and cook gently until done and add to any dish along with the cooking water.

Tomatoes can be used stewed or as tomato juice in any dish. Creamed corn is easier to feed than niblets.

Use **onions** and **garlic** as much as you can for their blood purifying effects and to help get rid of worms.

Herbs

Juliette de Bairacli Levy in her *The Complete Herbal Book for the Dog* regards herbs as a small but important part of a dog's diet, but as having a large part in animal medicine.* She feeds one dessert spoonful (½ tablespoon) of finely minced raw green celery, watercress, parsley, mint, or dandelion to her dogs with their daily meals. She also has pioneered the use of seaweed or kelp for not only dogs, but for cattle, sheep, goats, poultry and racing pigeons. Another thing she uses is flour from tree barks such as slippery elm, combined with other toasted flours and herbs, this is made into gruel with milk and is good for weaning pups, kittens and babies alike.

Herbal remedies and other Natural Rearing Products formulated by Juliette de Bairacli Levy are now available in the United States at Starfire Herb Co.

> *Natural Rearing Products*
> *5733 Guadalupe Trail N.W.*
> *Albuquerque, N.M. 87107*
> *Telephone: (505) 344-4503.*

You can write or phone for a list of products

If you have a drawer or shelf full of dried herbs you will never use before they are too old or stale, a way to put them to good use is to put a pinch or a teaspoonful in you pet's food every day. Crumble it up or grind in a blender for easier digestion. I put 1 tablespoon each of dried parsley, thyme, nettles and raspberry leaves in the supplement formula on page 99.

Some of the herbs you can use this way are:

nettles

raspberry leaves

peppermint

yarrow

sage

lemonbalm

dandelion

fenugreek

red clover

blackberry leaves

lovage

thyme

basil

linden flowers

rose hips

comfrey leaves & roots

fennel seeds

oregano

marjoram

rue

savory

southern wood

camomile

scullcap

parsley

caraway seeds

When your dried herbs are too old or stale to do anything else with, Ms. Levy suggests you grind them up and put them around your house or garden plants.

3rd 6/0
8-27-91
aj. didn't care for this but I thought it was really good!

CELEBRATIONS!

Party Mackerel or Salmon Loaf

      1 lb. can jack mackerel or salmon
      ½ cup sour cream or thick yogurt
      2 teaspoons dried parsley
      2 tablespoons wheat germ
      1 tablespoon chopped green pepper
      2 tablespoons chopped celery leaves or
         alfalfa sprouts
      1 tablespoon chopped onion
      1 egg
      1 tablespoon brewers yeast

Mix the salmon or mackerel with all other ingredients except the sour cream or yogurt. Don't remove any bones you find as these are soft and won't cause any trouble. Place in a casserole. Spread sour cream or yogurt on top and bake at 350° for 20 minutes. Serve with whole wheat biscuits or toast.

This can also be served unbaked. Heap the above ingredients into a mound and cover with sour cream.

You and your pets may share this nutritious dish with relish on any happy occasion.

73

Carrot Peanut Cake

For your dog's Birthday Celebration

>   1 cup whole wheat flour
>   1 teaspoon baking soda
>   1 tablespoon soy flour
>   ¼ cup chopped peanuts
>   1 egg
>   ¼ cup oil
>   1 teaspoon vanilla
>   ⅓ cup honey
>   1 cup ground carrots

Mix dry ingredients together. Add the rest of the ingredients. Mix together quickly and bake in a greased ring mold at 325° for 40 minutes.

If you have a blender, use it to grate the carrots by putting the egg and oil in first and then adding small pieces of carrot one at a time.

Catfish Pie

A party dish for 3 little kittens or any number you own

>   ½ cup oatmeal
>   ½ cup bran
>   ¼ cup wheat germ
>   ⅛ cup corn oil
>   ¼ cup soy flour

Mix ingredients together and press into small pie dish. Pyrex is best. Place in ice box until ready to use.

>   ½ lb. catfish fillets
>   2 eggs
>   1 cup milk or stock
>   1 tablespoon spinach
>   small pinch garlic
>   1 teaspoon parsley
>   ¼ teaspoon kelp

Cut fish up into pieces and arrange in pie crust. Mix milk or stock in a blender with egg, spinach, parsley, garlic and kelp. Pour over the fish in the pie shell and bake at 350° for ½ hour. Cool and serve upside down—crust on top.

Protein 32%   Fat 31%   Carbohydrate 37%

RECIPES FOR CATS & DOGS ON SPECIAL DIETS

Mark Morris, DVM, has saved the lives of countless dogs and cats by formulating specialized foods for pets who have diagnosed diseases. These canned foods are available only through veterinarians for the management of a disease or condition.

Most ailments or conditions, except perhaps overweight, should be properly diagnosed and your veterinarian's advice should be followed before you put your pet on any diet.

What I am doing here is giving information and recipes where possible, to help alleviate various problems that a change in diet might affect. A lot of health problems are food-oriented. I am not prescribing treatment but sharing things I have learned that seem sensible to me. If your pet does have an illness I suggest you discuss these ideas on diet with your veterinarian.

Basic Low Calorie Diet — For One Dog

This is a high protein meal for a dog whose ideal weight is 30 lbs., but who weighs a few lbs. more than that. Adjust the amount fed up or down according to the ideal weight of your pet. This is all you feed each day until the weight is off. If you notice that his coat is dull looking, add a teaspoon or two of corn oil. For a cat this recipe should be enough for about two days, but use about ⅔ of the cereal and vegetables.

> ¼ lb. ground lean beef, horsemeat* or fish
> ½ oz. beef liver
> ½ cup bran
> 3 tablespoons soy flour or 1 egg with shell pulverized in a blender
> 1 cup rolled oats, barley, (not pearled) cornmeal, or ½ cup rice
> ¼ cup powdered skim milk
> 2 tablespoons left over vegetables— preferably greens
> 1 teaspoon cod liver oil and wheat germ oil mixed
> 1 teaspoon kelp
> 1 tablespoon brewers yeast
> 1 teaspoon bone meal

Boil 3 cups water, add cereal grains and soy flour and simmer covered. When almost done, add bran, powdered skim milk, and wheat germ. Stir, add more water if necessary, and finish cooking. Add meat, liver and kelp. When cool enough to serve, add the vegetables and brewers yeast. If the vegetables need to be cooked, you can add them with the cereal.

*I don't like using horsemeat for mostly emotional reasons, but it is very lean.

Calories 958   Protein 33%
Fat 15%   Carbohydrate 52%

A Bland Diet For A Pet With A Food Allergy

> ¼ lb. chicken or ground lamb or mutton—
>   not too fat
> ½ cup converted rice
> 1½ cups boiling water
> 1 tablespoon corn oil
> ½ teaspoon sea salt
> ½ teaspoon bone meal
> a multiple vitamin supplement for dogs or cats

Lightly cook the meat in the oil. Cook the rice in the boiling water to which salt has been added. Add bone meal, and when cooled, add vitamin supplement, and mix with the meat.

If your pet seems well for a period of time, ask your veterinarian about adding one at a time, 1 oz. liver, brewers yeast, cooked carrots; green vegetables, ¼ cup corn meal or fresh corn, 1 teaspoon alfalfa, ½ cup soy grits and other kinds of meat.

Foods For A Low Sodium Diet

The Ritz diet (p 83) is a good low sodium diet. Never let your pet share your snacks such as potato chips, pop corn, (homemade unsalted is O.K.) pretzels, crackers, processed cheese, processed meats such as hot dogs, ham, bologna, salted peanuts, cottage cheese, bacon, salted butter & margarine, canned meat dishes, even canned baby meats. Avoid organ meats, egg whites, and salt water fish.

Foods low in sodium are horsemeat, lamb, beef, chicken, freshwater fish, egg yolks, milk, oatmeal, corn, rice, barley, wheat, soybeans and unsalted oils and fats.

If your pet has a heart condition the need for vitamin B complex is increased, so do give a 30 lb. dog 2 teaspoons of brewers yeast daily, even though it does contain some sodium. Instead of bone meal which has only a trace of sodium you might want to substitute a calcium salt like calcium lactate or dicalcium phosphate, but I wouldn't. I would give some lecithin every day (1 teaspoon).

Diarrhea & Vomiting

If severe, withhold food for a day or so, then feed barley water, or milk of oats with honey. If he holds these, slowly introduce solid food such as cottage cheese, rice, oatmeal and eggs.

Loss of Appetite and Fasting

When your cat or dog is ill and doesn't eat his food my suggestion is do not force it on him unless he is about to die of starvation. An ailing animal will usually fast in order to allow his body to recover. It has been found in one study that the presence of amino acids (from eating proteins) prevents the body from producing inteferon, a substance which fights virus organisms.

The remarkable Juliette de Bairacli Levy is very positive about the necessity of letting an animal fast when sick. In her book on natural rearing, *the Complete Herbal Book For The Dog* she says

"I often feel when thinking back on my canine work, that if I am able to instill two reforms into the canine world: the fasting of all dogs in sickness, and the strict feeding of raw flesh—never cooked meat in any form—then my years of canine work will not have been wasted ones."

78

She outlines in her book a program of fasting and recommends all or part of it for almost all sicknesses from worms to distemper.

Diet For An Older Animal

Older animals often suffer from such ailments as arthritis, heart conditions, coughs (which also may mean heart troubles), kidney failures, leaking in spayed females (ask your veterinarians for hormones to stop this), tumors, and bad teeth. Except perhaps for the leaking, most of these conditions can be improved or eliminated by proper diet. Raw or slightly cooked liver, brewers yeast, lecithin, kelp, bran, eggs with their shells pulverized, wheat germ, alfalfa, wheat germ oil, and cod liver oil should all be included in the daily diet, which should consist of high quality protein and good energy foods.

General Formula For An Older Dog's Dinner

½ oz. liver
¼ lb. lean meat or fish
⅓ cup dry rice, brown or converted
½ cup cornmeal or 1 cup creamed corn
2 tablespoons chopped cooked vegetables
1 teaspoon diced parsley or other herb or fresh
   herbs chopped fine
garlic and/or onions to taste
1 tablespoon corn oil
1 egg with shell

*1 teaspoon bone meal or 1 tablespoon
   calcium lactate
*1 tablespoon bran (unprocessed type from
   health food store)
1 tablespoon wheat germ
*1 teaspoon kelp
*1 tablespoon brewers yeast
*½ tablespoon lecithin
*1 teaspoon alfalfa powder (optional)
*¼ teaspoon magnesium oxide or epsom salt
1 teaspoon cod liver oil and wheat germ oil
   mixed

Cook the rice and cornmeal, or if you are using creamed corn, add it to the cooked rice. Put the egg with its shell in the blender to pulverize it and add it to the hot rice in order to cook it. Lightly cook the meats in the oil (if your pet can eat them raw so much the better). Add them to the mixture above along with the supplements.

Protein 26%   Fat 19%   Carbohydrate 55%

All the starred * ingredients can be mixed in quantity and added all at once. The wheat germ, however, should be kept in the refrigerator.

Geriatric Vitamin Mix

> 1 cup bran
> (1 cup wheat germ) keep this out unless you
>   refrigerate the whole thing
> 1 cup brewers yeast
> ½ cup lecithin
> 2 cups calcium lactate
>   or
> ½ cup bone meal
> ⅓ cup kelp
> ⅓ cup alfalfa
> 4 teaspoons magnesium oxide

Mix together and add ¼ cup for an average size dog's dinner. For a cat, use one tablespoonful.

Dinner For An Older Cat

Use the formula for the older dog dinner, but cut the amounts of rice, corn, vegetables and herbs in half.

These meals are high in nutrition and energy as well as fiber and ash. They should be fine for moderately healthy older pet, but if for any reason your pet cannot tolerate much fiber or ash, these meals should be modified accordingly.

Bladder And Urinary Problems

This stubborn condition happens to so many animals, especially cats, including mine, I want to share some of the information I have gathered on how diet may be of help. As you will see there is no agreement among the experts here either, and nothing has been proved conclusively. You will notice that your cat has a problem if he or she, although previously trained, starts urinating in various places, even when, or especially when you are watching, as if to tell you all is not well. Not much urine is passed, even after a long sitting, and it is frequently bloody. (This is not to be confused with the spraying of an unneutered male cat or the leaking of a spayed female dog. In the case of the spraying male cat, castrating is the answer, and a veterinarian can give your female dog hormone pills to control leaking).

When you first notice symptoms, see your vet, then see if any of the following suggestions will help.

First of all, encourage your cat or dog to drink more water. This can be done by adding an extra pinch of salt or salt substitute to their food. This should make him or her thirstier and increase the flow of urine.

If you are not giving a magnesium supplement (see chapter on supplements) start using one, and if you are, increase it. Dolomite tablets could be helpful. Along with the magnesium, give Vitamin B6 supplement, 5-10 Mg. for cats, up to 25 mg. for dogs every day. Be sure they are getting brewer's yeast at the same time. This careful use of minerals B6 and Yeast is recommended by Adele Davis* and others.

*Adele Davis "Lets Eat Right To Keep Fit"

Mr. and Mrs. Joseph Ritz of McAdoo, Pennsylvania have gone a different route. They have worked out a diet to relieve or control a urinary obstruction in their cat. He had had about 20 operations in one year and the veterinarian didn't give him much chance to live. He suggested they stop feeding him pet foods and milk. So on a trial and error basis, they evolved this diet. In four years no more attacks occurred and the Ritzes are very proud of their healthy beautiful cat.

This diet is being studied by the Mark Morris Animal Foundation in Topeka, Kansas. The basic idea is to restrict the ash content and minerals which could be stone formers. Here it is, just as they gave it to me. It should be all right for dogs too, if the quantities are increased.

Diet To Relieve Urinary Obstruction
by Mr. and Mrs. Joseph D. Ritz

Serve 3 or 4 Tablespoons of any of the following 3 or 4 times a day.

1. *Chicken Stew*—Steam 2 chicken breasts for about 1 hour (adding water as needed to make a broth) or use any chicken parts, if your cat will eat dark meat (mine won't). When meat is about ¾ done add 1 diced carrot and 1 diced potato, cook until tender. Mash potato and carrot in broth when done and chop chicken fine or grind and mix together. Make sure all bones and skin are removed. At each serving add a little warm water or heat with water on stove to serve at room temperature.

2. *Beef Stew*—Buy lean beef cubes. Braise meat

in water about 2 hours or until tender. Add carrot and potato or rice or any *fresh* vegetable your cat likes. Process as chicken stew.

3. *Liver*—Buy beef liver or occasionally chicken liver. Cook in water until well done about ½ hour. Chop in small pieces or grind. This can be served warm or at room temperature.

4. *Trout*—or any *fresh water* fish. Serve no salt water varieties. Bake about 20 min. clean out all bones and skin, flake into small pieces. This can be served at room temperature or slightly warmed with water and drained.

5. *Vegetables*—Corn on the cob, red beets, cabbage, cauliflower, broccoli. Buy only fresh vegetables. Cook until well done as you would for yourself. Cook *each* separately at varied times and serve no more than 1 or 2 servings per day. Make the other 2 meals meat or meat stews, or fish. Remove corn from cob before serving. Cut other vegetables into bite size pieces. If you have difficulty getting your cat to eat plain vegetables, try putting in a little meat broth with each serving.

6. Roast beef, steak, lamb, cabbage rolls stuffed with ground beef (if you grind your own), can also be served as tid bits from your meal if the food it *not* salted or seasoned.

Occasionally* as a snack, pop corn without salt or butter, dessicated liver tablets, garlic and parsley tablets, carob covered soy beans, raisins

*Occasionally, in this instance, means only 3 or 4 times a year. Absolutely no milk or dairy products or salt or sodium of any kind should ever be served.

or a *little* piece of angel food cake, can be given the cat. These are not meals, just treats and should only be served *after* he shows improvement from urinary problems.

I would like to add a few more suggestions for bladder ailments from Juliette De Bairacli Levy's *The Complete Herbal Book For The Dog*.

First, she says the roots of couch or quack grass possess remarkable stone-dissolving properties. She bruises two ounces of the root, pours 1½ cups boiling water on it and simmers it until one cup liquid remains. Allow to stand four hours, and morning and night give one to four tablespoons to your dog before meals. How much depends on the size dog you have. A cat can be given up to one tablespoon. Couch or quack grass is a favorite for nibbling by most pets. So if you have a yard full of it as I do, it is nice to know that this mean, impossible weed is good for something.

Ms. Levy also adds one teaspoonful of honey to one cup of barley water (see chapter V) to give soothing relief to bladder disorders. She tells of a Chow dog who was so ill with kidney trouble, he was given up as a hopeless case by the veterinary surgeon. She treated him by giving him parsley water three times a day along with milk and barley water sweetened with honey. He made a complete recovery and became a most beautiful and much photographed dog. Chopped raw parsley was added to all his meals the day he started to eat solid food and continued for the rest of his life.

Spring greens, such as asparagus, nettles and dandelion leaves are excellent cleansers for the urinary system.

IV HOW TO USE COMMERCIAL PET FOODS

I doubt if people would have pets in the numbers they do if it weren't for the convenience of commercial pet foods and the attractive commercials that go with them. But there are some pitfalls in using a purely commercial diet. On the following pages I will try to help you avoid some of these.

First of all, don't open a can of meat or fish and feed it daily without adding dry food or kibble. There are some brands of canned food that are combinations of meat and cereals and are labeled "balanced" or "complete," but these also are much better combined with a dry food to give the meal crunchiness and make it a more palatable meal as well as exercise your pet's teeth and jaws. An all meat diet, as I mentioned in the introduction, can seriously harm a pet, and even kill a kitten or puppy. Skin eruptions, bloody diarrhea, painful and weak joints, and soft bones are some of the problems that occur. The main reason for this is a lack of calcium. The balance of calcium to phosphorus should be about one to one but meat averages 20 or more times as much phosphorus as calcium. The proportion of meat to dry meal should be one of meat to four of the dry food. Bone meal should be added to insure that there is enough calcium and giving a large raw meaty bone every so often will help too.

Many dry foods are also labeled "complete" or "balanced." All the essential elements known to medical science are put in as you can see by reading the label. So what else is needed? Well, for one thing, fat is needed, as the makers cannot put enough fat in without it going rancid or bleeding through the bag. Fat can be added by pouring your leftover gravy over the dry food or using bacon fat, beef or chicken fat or any good unsaturated oil such as corn, safflower, or olive oil. It would be good to use fats and oils alternately. Of course part of the oil can be in the form of cod liver oil and wheat germ oil. As you know, too much fat will cause your pet to put on weight or it may fill him up before he has had enough food to nourish him properly. Dr. Donald R. Collins* recommends one tablespoon of oil or fat per day for a large dog. A cat would require up to one teaspoon depending on his size.

Dr. Collins has several chapters in his book on how commercial pet food is made and how to evaluate it. I recommend it highly. He suggests rinsing the gravy from canned food and seeing exactly what is left. It could be a shock. He recommends staying away from the very cheap brands as there is no way to make a food

*The Collins Guide to Dog Nutrition

that will nourish a dog for one or two cents a pound which is all that is left after canning and other expenses. Also look at the water content. If it is over 75% it is not a good buy. The very best canned food is labeled "Packed under continuous inspection of the United States Department of Agriculture."

One ingredient in pet foods I try to avoid is "by-products." There is no way of knowing just what this means in any particular food. Theoretically it consists of the clean, wholesome innards of animals such as lungs, stomach, intestines, brains etc. However in practice, "by-products" can include a lot of gristle, tails, trachea, hairs and meat from rejected or condemned animals known as 4-D animals—dead, dying, diseased, or disabled. By-products can even come from unwanted pets, the animals destroyed at humane societies. Until the labels can say clearly what by-products really are, we'll never know just what we are feeding our pets.

Semi-moist food in packages is high in protein, convenient to use, and cats and dogs seem to like it. In fact they become quite addicted to it, so what's the problem? Well, as I mentioned in the introduction, becoming addicted to any one food is unhealthy no matter how fortified it is, and these foods while good in some ways have some drawbacks and dangers as a steady diet.

One reason for the addiction is that most semi-moist food is about one-fourth sugar. If you were fed something that tasted like dessert every meal you would be loath to give it up too.

I happen to be of the opinion that sugar is bad for animals and people. It forms tartar on teeth, it can bring on diabetes or hypoglycemia, it can fatten your pet and at the same time not nourish him. There is no nutritional need for sugar, and in semi-moist foods most of the carbohydrates present are not in the form of wholesome cereal grains, but as sugar.

The reason the sugar is put in, is not for the taste, but as a preservative along with sorbitol and propylene glycol. These are humectants which means they take up moisture in the mixture and keep it tied up so that bacteria needing moisture cannot grow and spoil the food. Sorbitol and propylene glycol also are used in the body as a sugar.

So in feeding semi-moist food, know what you are doing and in order to avoid hooking your pet on it, feed it in combination with dry foods, cereals and vegetables, and watch your pet's weight!

It is a fact of life these days that practically all commercial foods for pets as well as for humans contain additives, preservatives and dyes as well as contaminants from our polluted planet. It is very difficult to know how to deal with these things even if we read all the labels carefully. Everything that is put in may not be listed and those that are may not have much meaning for us. Some may be thought harmless now, but what of their long range effects, or the effects of several mixed together? It has been proved that the toxic effects of several irritants are not added up but are multiplied, and that the damage is cumulative.

The American Medical Association warned recently that persons who eat cat and dog food could be receiving toxic levels of lead. An official from the Pet Food Institute argued with this, not that the lead is not there in toxic levels, but that there is no evidence that people eat pet food!

There are standards for the producers of human foods to follow, although there are many people who think they don't go far enough. There are also standards that producers of pet foods must follow before they can label a food "balanced," "complete," "scientific," or "perfect," and labels must list ingredients in order of quantity—that means the ingredient there is most of is listed first and so on. But aside from that we just don't know very much. Not enough for me anyway.

Dr. Collins says in his book, *"Unfortunate-*

ly, the foremost concern of most dog food manufacturers is not nourishment, but palatability. Only by making a food that a dog eats ravenously, can makers be assured of resales of their food" and he also says *"The suburbanite house pet has replaced the farm dog as the poorest fed dog in America. Unlike their predecessors, today's poorest fed dogs are not underfed but overfed. The horror of it all is the fact that while they may be overfed and overweight, they may also be undernourished!"*

To conclude, commercial foods are good to use with the following precautions.

1. Never use canned meat as a steady diet. Use one-fourth meat to three-fourths dry food.

2. Always buy foods marked "balanced" or "complete." Beware of very cheap brands.

3. A diet consisting of mostly dry food should have oil or fat added. One tablespoon a day for a large dog, one teaspoon for a small dog or large cat. Some of this oil should be wheat germ oil and cod liver oil.

4. With a diet of dry or semi-moist food, water should be available at all times, not just at meal times.

5. Do not use one type food exclusively as your pet may become addicted to it. This is especially true of semi-moist foods.

6. Read labels and if you can, try to avoid by-products and preservatives.

7. Do not feed dog food to your cat as it does not contain enough protein to adequately nourish a cat.

V HOW TO SUPPLEMENT YOUR PET'S DIET

You can always use vitamin and mineral preparations for cats and dogs, but for some reason these are usually in tablet form and I could never get one down the gullets of four cats and two dogs every day. So I have found some very good and less expensive methods of fortifying foods. You will find most of these helpers used in the recipes. The amounts given produce results and are as accurate as I can figure out, using the reference material on animal nutrition available to me. I make no other claims. Use these suggestions as a guideline and adjust to your pets' needs.

1. Always use fresh *whole grain cereals* without preservatives. These and all the following supplemental foods can be found in health food stores, but if you can find an animal feed store in a rural or semi-rural area, you can buy most of them at a fraction of the cost.

93

2. *Brewers yeast* is an excellent source of vitamin B complex and a good protein. If you get it at a health food store, buy the cheapest kind. Animals don't mind the taste. It promotes growth and good functioning of organs and nerves, and gives a shiny coat. ¼ to ½ teaspoon per adult cat per day. 1 teaspoon to 1 tablespoon per dog. Sprinkle on the food.

3. *Cod liver oil* supplies vitamins A and D. This fish oil is still quite inexpensive and pets love it, and it is essential for good teeth and bones, skin and fur. ¼ to ½ teaspoon per adult cat; ½ to 1 teaspoon per adult dog, 3 or 4 times a week. Use less in the summer. Too much fish oil can cause a disease called steatitus in cats, especially if it becomes rancid. Keep it in the refrigerator. Vitamin E oil retards rancidity.

4. *Bone meal* supplies essential calcium for bones and teeth and for proper functioning of heart and nerves. Nature intended carnivorous animals to eat bones along with the meat, as well as the partially digested vegetables in the stomachs of their prey. Dogs and cats who live on cooked meat alone are not getting nearly the calcium they need. This can result in weakening and stiffening of the rear leg joints. *Calcium* has also been found to be an excellent sedative and pain killer. So if your pet is in pain or very stressed, give extra bone meal or calcium tablets. 1 teaspoon per dog; ¼ teaspoon per cat per day.

5. *Wheat germ oil, or vitamin E,* is held to be essential to the survival of young animals, helps growth, and maintains sound hearts and pituitary glands. Besides promoting fertility and more efficient lactation, it gives new life to old dogs and cats and has been instrumental in healing bone and muscle injuries. Last but not least, *Vitamin E* retards rancidity of fats and oils in food. Sprinkle a few drops over food. If you don't want to bother with the oil, use wheat germ.

6. *Alfalfa meal or powder* is not only good for cows, but also marvelous for your pets, and for people, too, as are all of these supplements. Alfalfa has every vitamin listed as well as minerals less readily available in other foods. It is the most convenient source of Vitamin K which is necessary for blood clotting. Dried alfalfa contains over 20% protein, which makes it a pretty good survival food.

7. *Kelp powder* is another inexpensive food loaded with vitamins and minerals. Use it as salt or along with sea salt. Kelp contains iodine, needed by the thyroid gland

to regulate metabolism. It is also a great source of potassium which dogs and cats need almost as much of as calcium.

8. *Epsom salts* is a source of *magnesium*, a necessary mineral along with calcium and potassium. It is helpful for bladder problems. *Magnesium oxide* powder can also be used. Just a pinch a day should be enough for your cat; two pinches for your dog.

9. *Powdered skim milk, powdered cottage cheese*, and *powdered whey*, are good supplements to provide calcium. However, whey is high in milk sugar or lactose which is harder to digest for many animals and can cause diarrhea. Powdered cottage cheese is excellent if you can find it. Bone meal is cheaper than all three and it has no lactose.

10. *Lecithin* comes from soybeans. It has been used for years to make ice cream and candy smooth and to prevent rancidity. It is an emulsifier and there is good reason to believe it keeps cholesterol and other fatty deposits from accumulating in the body. It does help to metabolize fats and is good for older pets especially as it aids in keeping their hearts healthy and their blood vessels clean.

11. *Bran:* Carnivores in the wilds get plenty of roughage from the pelts and feathers of their prey, so if your pet tends to be constipated, or even if he is not, bran is an excellent substitute. Just sprinkle a spoonful over each meal.

12. *Milk of oats or barley water* are both very nutritious and strengthening for very young, sick or convalescent animals. Pour 1 pint boiling water over ½ cup oats or barley and let stand several hours, or overnight.

13. *Vitamin C*—I almost didn't include this vitamin as dogs and cats do manufacture it in their own bodies, but when illness strikes, vitamin C given in the form of powdered rose hips has been very helpful. Apparently there are times when extra vitamin C is needed.

    In an article in *Prevention*, August, 1976, a veterinarian, Wendell O. Belfield, D.V.M. of San Jose, California has reported saving hundreds of hopelessly ill dogs by giving them massive doses of vitamin C in shots and by mouth in food. In just a day or two, animals suffering from distemper, bronchitis, influenza, cystitis, and many other infectious diseases show great improvement and inside a week are completely cured and sent home with some powdered vitamin C to add to their daily meals. Dr. Belfield has cured severe kidney stones in a 4 year old male cat by adding one to two grams (1000 to 2000 mgs) of vitamin C to his food daily. Even bone problems involving lack of collegen (vitamin C is essential in forming this connective substance) have yielded to vitamin C treatment. Dr. Belfield is convinced from his work that vitamin C will prevent hip displasia in dogs. He recommends adding powdered vitamin C daily to the food of all dogs and cats. He suggests three fourths to one and a half grams (750 to 1500 mgs.) for a small dog and up to six grams (6000 mgs.) daily for a large one. According to these doses, a cat would get about 500 to 1000 mg daily. He assures us that no side effects or toxicity have been observed. This seems like a large amount to me unless an illness is present. My cats have not eaten much of their food with one fifth of that much vitamin C added to it (ascorbic acid has a sour taste). It may take some getting used to. I do believe supplementing with vitamin C will be very useful especially in the winter. Try ground rose hips.

A letter writer to *Prevention* (July 1976) says she clears up summer rashes on her pet terriers by dusting them several times a day with a mixture of 500 mg crushed vitamin C, 2 tablespoons baking soda, and 2 tablespoons cornstarch. I tried it on myself and it really does stop itching from insect bites.

14. *Apple cider vinegar* treatment in Dr. Jarvis' book *Folk Medicine* has helped to relieve arthritis in both people and animals. It helps the body to absorb minerals better. One teaspoon per pint of drinking water has kept goats worm and lice free, it might do the same for a dog. It can also be added to the daily meals.

15. *Zinc* is a mineral that has recently been found to be lacking in food grown in the

U.S.A., but is essential enough to be added to most commercial cat and dog foods. Wounds, ulcers inside and outside the body, and painful joints are healed faster when zinc is present. It is helpful in heart conditions and may even help reduce doggie odors. A few zinc tablets crushed and added to the supplement below, may be just what your pet needs if he is not getting it from his food.

HOW TO MIX A VITAMIN AND MINERAL SUPPLEMENT

This sounds like a lot at first and it is, but it is well worth the trouble, and not bad after you get used to it. All the powders are mixed together and given all at once. The proportions I would suggest are:

2 cups brewers yeast
1 cup bone meal
¼ cup magnesium oxide powder
¼ cup alfalfa meal or powder
2 tablespoons kelp

Give ½ teaspoon per meal to your cat. ½ to 1 tablespoon per meal to your dog (average size).

99

Cod liver oil can be mixed with vitamin E oil. The average cat or dog should have approximately 30 I. U. vitamin E per day. So for each ½ teaspoon of cod liver oil, add the amount of vitamin E oil to equal 30 I. U., and use it as directed under cod liver oil.

One thing more, you will notice I use *sea salt* because it contains practically all the minerals known and unknown, in their original natural combination from the sea. *Kelp* has concentrated these elements and can be used instead of, or along with, sea salt, one tablespoon of kelp will substitute for one teaspoon of salt.

VI SOME NATURAL HOME REMEDIES FOR YOUR PETS

It is my feeling that left alone, animals instinctively know how to heal themselves and how to select the food they need if it is available. But our pets are always with us and have taken on some of our bad habits. If our cat or dog is ailing or has been hurt, not seriously, I wait to see if he can take care of it himself. Then I give what help I can and if that isn't enough, off to the veterinarian we go. Of course I believe in preventive shots and check-ups.

If your pet receives a shot of *antibiotics*, give him some *yogurt* to restore the friendly bacteria in his digestive tract. Antibiotics kill all bacteria—friendly as well as unfriendly.

Yogurt is also helpful if your dog or cat has *gas* and overwhelms you with odors. Again the need is to increase the friendly bacteria that digest food speedily before it putrefies. Putrification can be an indication of too much meat in the diet.

Again I want to mention Juliette De Baira-cli Levy's advice which says—*"Never force a sick animal to eat, as fasting is nature's way to heal."* In her books she outlines a complete program for curing many diseases by this method. If you want to try her ways, I suggest you study her books carefully, for *natural rearing* is a way of life and not really for treating symptoms.

Nevertheless there are many useful and helpful things to be learned about herb medicines from her books as well as from other sources so I would like to include a few of them. They are safe, harmless and often helpful.

For bathing *wounds* try *witch hazel* instead of iodine or make a strong tea from *rosemary* or *blackberry leaves:* add 2 teaspoons dried leaves to 1 cup boiling water and allow to steep several hours. Ms. Levy never has her dogs' wounds stitched up or bandaged unless they are very serious.

Many people keep an *aloe plant* and use its juice on *wounds* and *burns* as well as *rashes.*

Put *vitamin E oil* or *vitamin A ointment* on *burns, cuts, scrapes,* or even *warts,* for quick healing with no scars.

Also try *honey* on *sores, small wounds, burns* and *inflamed eye* rims when in your estimation they are not serious enough for a visit to the veterinarian. Roman soldiers carried honey into battles for first aid as well as good energy food. As a food, honey is quickly digested and is a tonic for the whole body. Put a little in the milk given to puppies, kittens, or any pet who is sick.

For *rashes or eczema* a tea of *blackberry leaves* and *red clover leaves and blossoms* or *elder flowers* is recommended by Ms. Levy. Bathe the area using absorbent cotton several times a day. Dab *insect bites* with *vinegar* to neutralize their sting. A cut *onion* rubbed on a *bite* is also a good remedy.

The ground root of *golden seal* is one of the best medicines in nature. A tea made of 1 teaspoon of *golden seal* in 2 cups of boiling water and allowed to steep for 20 minutes will heal *open sores, inflammations, eczema, ringworm* and any other *skin diseases*, according to Jethro Kloss in *Back to Eden**. Use it as a wash and sprinkle some of the powdered root on too. It can also be used in combination with powdered *myrrh*, that ancient Bible remedy, for *sore eyes, wounds* and *ulcers*. Add 1 teaspoon of myrrh to the boiling water with the *golden seal* above.

My daughter's amazing pet chicken, Felicia, regrew flesh, skin, and feathers after a horse had bitten a chunk out of her back. Debbie, my daughter, attributes this to the washing of Felicia's wounds with *golden seal* tea twice a day.

*Read this valuable book for many uses for golden seal and myrrh and much much more.

When your pet has *constipation or digestive problems*, do not feed any white flour or sugar but increase bulk and fiber by feeding baked or boiled potato skins and sprinkle raw bran flakes on the food every day. Make sure your pet is not anemic by giving enough iron in the form of raw liver, molasses, and even dried prunes, figs and raisins. Alfalfa in the form of tablets or flour is cleansing, and flax seed is a gentle bulk laxative. Carob also is a high fiber food. Give kaopectate for diarrhea.

Wild raspberry leaves dried and made into a tea have been given to *pregnant dogs* and women all over the world. The results have been amazing, in promoting the well being of the mothers and ease of deliveries. In fact many breeders have written to Ms. Levy to say that their dogs whelped so easily they considered it little short of miraculous. Tame or cultivated raspberry leaves are not as good as the wild variety, but can be used if free of spots and pesticides.

Golden seal and *myrrh* given internally will cure *coughs* and *colds*. As it is very bitter, wrap a small amount of the powder in ground meat or liver sausage or thick honey.

Coughing—One cold wintry night, our second night with our 18 month Labrador from the pound, she started to cough and spit up phlegm all over the place. I quickly consulted *The Complete Herbal Book For The Dog* for something to give her that I had in the house. Garlic, honey and oil of eucalyptus were indicated for bronchitis, pleurisy and pneumonia. Great, I had them so I took a garlic clove and flattened it slightly. I put 3 drops of eucalyptus oil on it and surrounded it with a teaspoon of honey, and fed it to her quickly. She coughed just once more after that but no phlegm. The next evening she started to cough again so I repeated the treatment and it was over—she never has coughed since. Ms. Levy says in her book that the action of garlic in the lungs is remarkable. It is indeed!

Fleas are terrible pests and the weaker an animal is, the more fleas he has. Flea season is a real drag, and is the time we are tempted to buy one of those flea collars. I have succumbed a couple of times until someone noticed the neck of our oldest Siamese cat was raw, running and ulcerated. We quickly removed all the collars and apologized to our pets. I really did know better than that. I knew for example that flea collars and no-pest strips contain a poison DDVP or dichlorvos that is a nerve gas and can be lethal to a cat, especially in hot weather.

If you do buy a *flea powder*, be sure you get one that is made of *pyrethrum* which are flowers called painted daisies and are related to chrysanthemums. The smell of pyrethrum is repellent to insects but harmless to animals and humans. These daisies, planted in your yard, will keep insects away. Powders or lotions containing rotenone (derris root) are also relatively safe.

Garlic powder sprinkled liberally and rubbed into your dog's fur will keep away fleas. A letter in *Prevention* magazine says that every two months or so the writer smears salad oil into a 6x10 inch area on the lower back of their large short haired dog. Then a heavy sprinkling of garlic powder is rubbed into the area. The dog smells like a walking salad dressing for a few hours, but it soon disappears and so do the fleas, completely, for 2 to 3 months.

Another *flea repellent* is penny royal, a mint. Oil of penny royal can be bought in a drug store and several drops rubbed on the fur will keep fleas away, if not get rid of them.

As I mentioned on page 61, one way to keep fleas off of your pet is to be sure he gets some brewers yeast every day, the stronger the flavor the better. If this doesn't work add some thiamine to it. Thiamine or vitamin B1 has a strong scent which fleas don't seem to like. Crush enough thiamine tablets to make 100mg. and add it to the supplement formula on P 99.

To get rid of the fleas that are there, a bath with a very foamy non-soap is safest and best. Fleas drown very easily and the foam helps to trap them. By non-soap I mean a soap made from a plant or bark that is naturally foamy, *not* a detergent.* If you must use a regular soap use the mildest kind you can find, as dogs and especially cats have very sensitive skins, and do it outside if possible with warm water on a hot sunny day.

Ticks are usually repelled by the same things that fleas are, but you may find one clinging to your pet by embedding its tiny head into the flesh. As it gorges itself on blood, it swells up until it looks like a brown or purple grape. My daughter gets it out head and all by holding it as near the head as possible and exerting a gentle but steady pull. Do not use matches or gasoline! Dab the spot with witch hazel on a piece of cotton if it bleeds. This whole process is painless.

To give a *dry shampoo* use *warm bran, oatmeal* or *cornmeal*. Warm it in the oven and try to keep it warm as you use it in order to dissolve the grease and dirt. Take only enough off the heat to do one section of your pet at a time. Rub it into the fur with a towel and brush it out.

For *worms*, I put as much *garlic* in the food as my pet will eat. If that doesn't work, put *garlic juice* in a dropper or squeeze bottle and squirt

*Canex Bathing Tablet is a soapless product containing natural tree oils and kills fleas by foamy suffocation. It is safe for cats or dogs. It is a Natural Rearing Product made by N E C A Products of Tel Aviv, Israel and can be bought from N.R. Products, The Hall, Kettlebastin, Suffolk, 1P7 7QA, England.

about one fourth teaspoon down his throat before he eats. If your pet will take pills, you can buy garlic perles in a health food store. Another good way to administer garlic, is to take one teaspoon of ground meat, flatten it out and put ¼ teaspoon garlic powder or a garlic clove in the center. Roll it into a ball and pop it into your pets mouth.

This *garlic* treatment is mostly a *worm preventive* for a relatively healthy animal. It probably won't work for one that is really infested. There are many types of worms and worm cures and I am not equipped to deal with them here. Unfortunately most of the cures do as much or more violence to the animal as the worms do. *The Complete Herbal Book For The Dog* does give some treatments that are natural and non-violent, and I recommend it. As worms are everywhere in the environment like bacteria, the best preventative is a healthy animal, as worms and germs like to feast on disease. The same is true for fleas.

One type of worm that you cannot avoid if infected mosquitos are in your area, no matter how healthy your dog is, is heartworm. We lost one of our dogs to this tragic disease last year. Actually I think she died from the treatment. I knew the medicine was a form of arsenic and I couldn't bring myself to have her examined for heartworm when I first heard that it was around. After all she was a longhaired dog and I didn't think of mosquitos biting her around the eyes and nose. Well, by the time I reconciled myself to doing something about it, she had several worms growing in her heart muscle, although no symptoms were present. She died three weeks after the treatment started of an internal hemorrhage, which I think was caused by the dead worms traveling through her blood vessels and causing one to burst. Her death was quick and seemingly painless, and we console ourselves with knowing that dying from heartworm disease would have been much worse. I tell you this to warn you not to put off treatment because the longer the worms are there, the bigger and more numerous they get. There is a real need for a less dangerous treatment for heartworm and a non-poisonous mosquito abatement program.

Most animals that are well fed and cared for will be healthy all their lives. Be sure WATER IS ALWAYS AVAILABLE.

VII AN INCREASE
IN THE FAMILY

A pregnant Mother dog requires more food and, of course, more supplements. I give extra brewers yeast, bone meal and ¼ teaspoon epsom salts, or a mineral supplement containing magnesium, every day. Also ¼ cup powdered skim milk or cottage cheese. If she gets diarrhea, use mostly bone meal. (See chapter on fortifying your pets diet.) It is a good idea, if you suspect worms, to put a garlic clove in her food once a week while pregnant, but don't do this when she is nursing!

After the puppies arrive, the mother dog should be fed two to three times as much food while she is nursing. Feed her twice a day.

If for some reason, heaven forbid, you must make puppy formula, here is one:

> 2 cups whole milk or 1 cup evaporated milk
> and 1 cup water
> 1 egg yolk, ¼ cup brewer's yeast
> 2 tablespoons cream or 1 tablespoon
> unsaturated oil
> ½ teaspoon bone meal

Protein 33%   Fat 38%   Carbohydrate 29%

Bitch's milk is 39% Protein, 46% Fat, 15% carbohydrate.

This is calculated without taking into account water or ash content. This looks like a very rich formula, but it isn't when compared to the bitch's milk calculated the same way.

Every couple of days add one or two drops of cod liver oil to the formula for each puppy. There is a product called Esbilac which is made for bottle feeding puppies.

Remember you are feeding infant animals who have not yet built up a resistance to diseases and are not getting any protection from mother's milk, so sterilize your equipment and wash your hands as you would for a human baby. Doll bottles with nipples will work quite well.

Dr. Donald R. Collins in *The Collins Guide to Dog Nutrition*, has an excellent chapter on caring for orphaned pups, and if you need it, I suggest you run, not walk, to the nearest library or bookstore to get a copy. He gives a formula for feeding puppies that works and is much simpler than mine. It is 3 parts of evaporated milk to one part of water. It is not as rich in protein and fat as the one above. Leaving out the water and ash content, it is 28% protein, 32% fat and 40% carbohydrate.

I was recently thrilled and very honored to receive from Juliette de Bairacle Levy personally, her recipe for hand rearing litters. It has always proved very successful. I give it to you just as she wrote it.

"Litters sometimes have to be hand-raised, all or several of the pups. The mother may have been weakened from a difficult whelping, or there may be one or two pups weaker than the rest and therefore not getting their fair share of food and needing helping out. Do NOT use dried or canned milk. Use freshly bottled cow's milk, or better use fresh goat's milk. Milk needs to be enriched to compare with the very rich milk of the canine race. For 7 hours before feeding, soak raw flaked oats or flaked oats and barley in the fresh (unheated) milk. To every half litre (pint) of milk, add one heaped teaspoon of flaked cereals per pup. Leave this to soak. Then strain off the cereal* and beat into the cereal-

---

**This oats residue can be fed to the mother to increase her milk. I do not think that this kind of oats or barley is available in this country. We would have to substitute instant oats or barley.*

enriched milk, two teaspoons of pure honey and the raw yolk of one egg. If obtainable also add a half teaspoon of almond oil. Mix very well and feed, gently warmed, in an infant's bottle. After each pup has fed, wipe the mouth clean with a damp cloth and support the pup upright on its haunches to pass 'wind' (in the same way as human babies are held up to pass wind after feeding.) When the puppies are several weeks old, thicken the milk with maize (corn) flour and herbs (such as provided by natural rearing gruel or other natural formula).

Two days per week omit the egg yolk to rest the digestion. Later, at four weeks, some molasses also can be added, a half teaspoon per pup."

During the second month, puppies can start being weaned. In any breed, growing pups need twice as much food as their parents and when between 7-9 weeks they need three times as much food. They should be fed THREE TIMES a day until six months old and then TWICE a day until eight months old after which once a day is fine.

For puppies first foods:

1. Baby cereal mixed with milk or soybean milk and chopped liver.
2. Meat soups with vegetables.
3. Big bones with meat.
4. Cooked whole grain cereals with milk or soybean milk.
5. Cottage cheese.
6. Cooked eggs.
7. Mashed vegetables such as potatoes, carrots, peas, beans, cauliflower, turnips, cabbage greens.
8. Cod liver oil brewers yeast and calcium supplements.

When Mama cat is expecting, the treatment should be the same as for Mother dog. Give her more food and brewers yeast, a pinch of Epsom salts, or a mineral supplement containing magnesium every day as well as foods containing calcium such as milk and cheese. Garlic is also recommended in case of worms. Try making a tea of a crushed clove of garlic and one half teaspoon sage in one half cup of boiling water and pour some of this over her food.

Cats generally have very strong maternal instincts so you can trust your cat to take excellent care of the kittens without much help from you. Just feed her well twice a day. When she wants to wean the kittens she may bring a piece of fish or liver to them. Then you can start feeding them too. I usually start offering solid food to them at four to five weeks and if Mama cat doesn't want them to have it she will eat it herself and then plop down and nurse them.

WATER SHOULD BE AVAILABLE AT ALL TIMES.

HERE IS A FORMULA for motherless kittens or you can buy a product which is similar to cat mother's milk called Esbilac.

> *2 cups whole milk or 1 cup evaporated milk
> and 1 cup water.*
> *2 egg yolks*
> *¼ cup brewers yeast*
> *¾ teaspoon bonemeal*

37% Protein   31% Fat   32% Carbohydrate
Mother cat or queen's milk.
41% Protein 29.5% Fat 29.5% Carbohydrate

Calculated on a dry basis leaving out water and ash content.

I was astonished at how high in protein and fat the milk of cats and dogs really is. It is very difficult to mix anything to get that much protein. Soybean milk has the highest protein content, but I haven't tried it for pups or kittens yet. It is worth trying, certainly.

Every day or so give each kitten one or two drops of cod liver oil in its milk.

116

As you probably know, the mother cat takes care of all the body wastes of the kittens by licking them after they are fed. So if you are feeding motherless kittens you'll have to take care of the other end too, by gently but firmly massaging the anal and urinary areas with a piece of damp cotton or tissue after each feeding.

Cat and dog milk is richer and less sweet than cow or human milk:

	Cat	Dog	Cow	Human	Goat
Water	82%	75%	87%	87.4%	86.8%
Protein	7%	8.4%	3.4%	1.3%	3.7%
Sugar	5%	3.2%	4.9%	7 %	4.6%
Fat	5%	9.8%	3.8%	3.5%	4 %
Ash	.6%	.7%	.7%	.2%	.8%

How Many Cats and Dogs Are Enough?

We found no way to live comfortably with our dogs and cats without having them spayed or castrated sooner or later. This is an expensive, and to most a traumatic and drastic measure. But up until now there has been no other rational choice, and the heartbreak of unwanted kittens and puppies is so terrible, we didn't want to add anymore to that population explosion. I fervently hope that some day a good method of birth control will be available that is more reasonable and easier for both the animal and his owner.

VIII – NAMING THE NEW ONES

They say that pets, especially cats, have a way of naming themselves. However, it helps to give them a name to start out with. Naming pets is usually a pleasant exercise, but sometimes it becomes a perplexing business. Kittens have gone nameless for weeks while we agonized over a decision. Once we held a naming contest among the family members and voted for the winner. When there is a litter of pups or kittens, it helps to give group names. For example, our five Siamese kittens were named after characters in the operetta *The Mikado*. They were called Poo Ba, Nanki Poo, Yum Yum, Koko, and Catishaw. Here are the names of all the pets I have known or have heard of.

Male Names

Abner	Baron	Busby
Adam	Bart	Buster
Agamotto	Basil	Byron
Aimless	Bear	
Alfred	Beethoven	Cadwallader
Algernon	Benji	Caesar
Alister	Bernard	Caleb
Alphonse	Bert	Calvin
Andy	Big Business	Captain America
Angus	Biggie	Captain Marvel
Archie	Black Angus	Captain Nemo
Arthur Peterson	Blue	Casper
Ashes	Blaze	Catastrophe
Ashley	Boeing	Caution
Asta	Bones	Cecil
Asterviel	Boots	Chico
Augustus	Boris	Chadwick
Attila	Bounce	Charlie
Atlas	Bowser	Charlie Chan
Attuma	Bozo	Chauncey
	Bruce	Christopher
Baldy	Bruno	Chou Chou
Barnaby	Brutus	Chumley

Claude
Cognac
Comet
Cornelius
Cream
Cupid
Curry
Cyclops
Cyprus

Delaware
Dexter
Diablo
Dionysius
Dormammu
Dracula
Dr. Strange
Dudley
Dundee

Earl Grey
Ebenezer
Edsel
Ellery Queen
Elmer
Elton
Emil
Emmanual
Ernest
Eros
Eustace

Fang
Fargo
Fearless
Feckless
Felix
Ferdinand
Fidel
Fido
Flash Gordon
Friskie
Fuzzy Face

Gabriel
Garcia
Gaspar
George
Giles
Godfrey
Gotcha
Groucho
Grover
Gulliver

Hamlet
Hannibal
Hans
Happy
Harvey
Havok
Hector
Hercules
Herman
Hobart
Horatio
Hugh
Humphrey

Ichabod
Inkie
Ira
Ivan

Jack
Jarvis
Jason
Jasper
Jeramiah Kitten
Joe
Joe's Grocery
Jonathan
Josh
Julius

Kang
Ka-Zar
Kassimer

Kemosabi
Killer
King
King Kong
Koko
Krushchev
Kukla

Lafayette
Lancelot
Larry
Leander
Lei Kung
Leo
Leon
Leonidas
Lieutenant Kiji
Linus
Lionel
Loki
Lucifer

Mai Ling
Major Grey
Mandrake
Manfred
Marcus
Marmaduke
Mars
Martin
Matchu
Matt Dillon
Maurice
Mickey
Midas
Midnight
Mincemeat
Ming the Merciless
Mister Gray
Mongul
Mordo
Mordred
Morris
Mu

Namor
Napoleon
Narcissus
Nelson
Neptune
Nestor
Nick
Night Crawler
Night Country
Nudge

Obadiah
Oberon
Octavius
Oliver
Orion
Oscar
Osirus
Otis
Otto
Owen

Panda
Panther
Perly
Piglet
Piner
Pluto
Pogo
Pointless
Pokey
Poo Ba
Pooh Bear
Pooka
Popeye
Prince
Pumkin

Quasimodo
Quentin
Quicksilver
Quidnunc
Quinsy

Rags
Rajah
Ralph
Randolph
Ranger
Rasputin
Ratso
Remus
Rex
Reynold
Rigel
Roger
Roger Wilco
Roland
Rollo
Romulus
Rosco
Rover
Rudolph
Rufus

Sam
Sambo
Sampson
Schweppes
Sebastian
Senator
Sequoia
Severin
Shep
Sherlock
Siegfried
Silas
Silver
Silvester
Simon
Sinbad
Sirius
Sir Viver
Sooty
Sparks
Sparky
Spock

Spot
Stewart
Stripes
Sugar
Summa

Tantalus
Tarzan
Tasha
Taylor
Terry
Tex
Thor
Timothy
Titus
Tiger
Tobias
Toby
Tobomory
Tom
Tonto
Tony
Topper
Towser
Trash
Tuey

Ulysses
Underdog
Uriah
Uru

Valentino
Victor
Virgil
Vishtar
Vulcan

Wags
Wen Chang
Wilber
Whizzer
Wolf

Xanthos

Xavier
Xerox
Xerxes

Yang
Yen Lo
Yuba

Zachary
Zane Grey
Zarathustra
Zarkov
Zemo
Zeus
Zoroaster

Feminine Names

Abby
Amelia
Andromeda
Angel
Antoinette
Aphodite
Ariadne
Astra
Aura
Aurelia

Balinka Wozney
Bastet
Bella
Belle
Berenice
Bertha
Bessie
Beula
Biri
Brigid
Brunhilda
Buffy
Butterfly

Candy
Calypso

Carbonelle
Carmella
Carmen
Casseopia
Cecily
Celeste
Chanel
Chang Hsien
Charli
Charo
Chloe
Christabel
Cinde
Circe
Clarrisse
Cleopatra
Clementine
Clothilde
Coco
Concordia
Constance

Dagmar
Daisy Mae
Dale Ardon
Daphne
Delia
Delilah
Della
Dinah
Dora
Drusilla
Duchess
Dulce

Edwina
Electra
Eloise
Emma
Emily
Enchantress
Ermengarde
Estelle

Etta
Eudora
Eulalie
Eve

Felicia
Fiscal
Fizz
Flavia
Freya
Fricka
Fruma Sarah
Fuji

Geraldine
Gilda
Ginger
Graceless
Greta
Griselda
Guinevera
Guttersnipe
Gwendoline

Harlequin
Harpie
Harriet
Heidi
Hela
Henrietta
Hera
Hilda
Hildegarde
Hippolyta
Hortense
Hsi Wang Mu
Hyacinth

Imogene
Ina
India
Ishtar
Isis
Isabel
Izanami

Jenny
Jinca
Jitterbug
Junebug
Juno

Kali Fi
Kalua
Kanga
Karma
Kamilla
Kiki
Kingu
Kitty
Kwan Yin

Lady
Lady Jane
Laila
Leda
Leila
Lei Tsu
Lena
Letitia
Lieutenant Uhura
Lilith
Little
Lola
Loma
Lucretia Borgia
Luna
Lydia

Macha
Madame Butterfly
Madame Curie
Madeline
Maia
Marshmallow
Mata Hari
Maybelline
Medusa
Mercedies
Mignon

Milly
Minerva
Minnie
Missie
Mitzie
Moet
Moira
Moondragon
Morgan le Fay
Morrigan
Myrtle

Nannette
Naomi
Narda
Narley
Natasha
Nebula
Nefertiti
Nell
Netti
Ninkur
Niobe
Nymph

Pandora
Pang
Pansy
Persephone
Ping
Pongee
Portia
Prism
Prudence
Psyche
Putana
Python

Octavia
Odette
Olga
Oline
Olive

Olympia
Ondine
Onyx
Oops
Opal
Ophelia
Orient
Ouija

Queenie
Quidame
Quinine
Quinquina

Raquel
Raven
Ravinia
Regina
Renpet
Rococo
Rosamund
Rosetta
Rowena
Roxy
Rubella
Ruby

Sabina
Sally
Salome
Sayonara
Scheherazade
Senorita
Serpent
Shanna
Shasha
Siren
Snowbia
Star
Sugarplum
Suzanne Fox
Sybil
Sylvia

123

Tabitha
Tash Mahal
Tashmit
Tattoo
Thalia
Thomasina
Tigress
Tinkerbelle
Titania
Toffee
Topaz

Ulrica
Umar
Una
Undine
Urania
Ursula
Utopia

Valeria
Valkyrie
Vanessa
Varuni
Velvet
Venus
Verushka
Vienna
Vina
Violet
Vivicious
Vixen
Voodoo
Vulpecula
Vulpina

Wanda
Whilhelmina
Wicked

Winifred
Winkie
Woozi

Xanadu
Xenia

Yin
Yeta
Yoyo

Zelda
Zenobia
Zephyr
Zoe

IX FURTHER NOTES AND DEFINITIONS *not fully covered in the other chapters*

Ash is what is left after a food has been burned in an oven. Too much ash has been considered undesirable and as it is associated with kidney stones and bladder infections, many people look for low ash content when they buy pet food. However, Dr. Jim Corbin in *Nutrition of Cats* says that ash includes practically all the minerals needed for normal body functions and is quite necessary for health. After all, ash contains calcium, potassium, magnesium, sodium and all the trace minerals.

Kittens fed a diet of 30% ash did not get kidney stones and although cats fed a commercial food high in ash did show some deposits in their kidneys, these were thought to be caused mainly by a lack of Vitamin B6 or pyroxidine in their diet.*

*Nutrient Requirements of Domestic Animals Number 10, National Research Council.

Fiber is the undigestible part of grains and other foods. It was thought that fiber had little value as food and it still is systematically removed from grains and flours. Low fiber or low residue were prescribed for intestinal problems like diverticulitus, colitus, diarrhea and constipation. Now fiber is used to prevent these same problems because it helps stimulate the intestines to do their work and is necessary for proper elimination. Animals in the wild state get plenty of fiber from eating the pelts of their prey. We can give our pets more fiber by adding wheat bran rice bran, alfalfa and carob.

Litter And Litter Boxes Most people use a commercial kitty litter and it works quite well in a rectangular plastic dishpan, as long as you remove the solids and change it often. Used litter can be put in a compost heap or garden as long as your soil needs clay, as that is what it is. If your soil has too much clay to begin with, do not use it.

I have been using sawdust in my litter boxes mixed with commercial litter—just enough to give it some weight so that it doesn't fly around and so that the box does not tip over when a cat perches on the edge. Sawdust is marvelously deodorant, absorbant, available in any lumberyard or shop, and it is *free!* You might want to use a box with higher sides such as a baby bathtub to keep it from scattering. I don't mind if it does scatter as it is a very good sweeping compound. Used sawdust can be used as mulch or compost, but it is acid and unless you need acid in your soil, must be used along with lime.

Granulated peat moss can also be used as litter and when used, is all right to put in the garden as a mulch or compost. The feces and urine will not hurt the soil but if you have qualms about it, put your used litter on a compost heap.

Accidents On The Rug Or Floor. These are best gotten rid of immediately, but because I am still somewhat squeamish, I remove as much as I can with newspapers and spread sawdust or litter on the remaining spot. This will dry and deodorize it, and can be vacuumed up later. Of course there is no substitute for scrubbing with soap or detergent and water and the litter or sawdust can be sprinkled on afterwards to dry a thick rug or carpet. The way to kill any remaining odors and to discourage your cat from reusing a forbidden spot is to spray it with vinegar or a dilute solution of formaldehyde.

A letter to *The Mother Earth News* No. 41 says sprinkling some ground cloves on the area will also do the trick and it certainly smells better than formaldehyde.

Dishes. The ideal dishes for dogs and cats are pyrex glass, stainless steel or procelain bowls that won't tip over, and do not have cracks or chips that will collect bacteria. Use your old bowls and plates or buy some in a second hand store. Cats have traditionally used saucers, as most families have some left after the cups have been broken. All dogs and cats I know prefer their own individual plates. Sharing a bowl may look cute, but it makes most animals nervous and they may eat too fast and throw it up later.

I prefer porcelain or glass because, while pottery is very good and is made into ideal heavy feeding bowls, it is just possible that the glaze contains lead. I don't know this for a fact, but it wouldn't hurt to ask before your purchase one. Remember dogs and cats have sharp teeth.

Stainless steel feeding bowls are excellent, easy to keep clean, unbreakable and don't tip over. The only drawback here is the cost, but they do last forever. Stainless steel bowls have one great advantage. They can be put on top of the stove and warmed so that food doesn't have to be served cold.

I do not like aluminum or plastic bowls as they are likely to be dented or shredded by an animal's strong teeth. In addition, although we may not notice it, a dog or cat's sensitive nose may detect and dislike a chemical odor in the plastic.

For young kittens, I wash and use flat cat food cans for milk as nothing can tip them over.

Introducing A New Pet. A new kitten or puppy will not cause much consternation among the other pets you may have, but introducing an adult dog or cat is often difficult. My three cats lived on top of the refrigerator for three weeks before they got used to having a dog in the house, and for the dog to calmly accept them.

Our most recent dog, Charlie, a 1½ year old female lab-shepherd reacted hysterically to our cats, and although they were used to dogs by then, they all beat a hasty retreat to various shelves and cabinet tops. So we had to keep Charlie in a separate room. I read in *Cat Breeding and General Management* by P.M. Sodenberg that the way to introduce animals to each other is to first separate them and then have the separated pets change rooms every so often so that they will get used to each others' smells.

We did this for the first week, then we brought my daughter's young and fearless kitten, Ellery Queen, or our old and completely imperturable cat, Pooh Bah, into the room with Charlie, letting one of them sit on the top of the dishwasher out of reach of an hour or two. Last we brought Charlie held tightly on a leash into the room with all the cats, making sure they had places to retreat to. Finally after two weeks of this, Charlie learned not to bark and chase them and we all breathed easier. We thought it would never happen.

How To Give A Pill. Open your pet's mouth and put it on the back of the tongue, shut and hold the jaws together until it is swallowed. I am not good at this so I resort to the following subterfuges.

1. I wrap it in something tasty and hand feed it. This works for dogs but not often with cats. I also put it on the floor wrapped or unwrapped and hope curiosity will do the trick.

2. I bury it in the food and hope it isn't noticed and spit out.

Traveling. There are quite a few books written on how to take your pet on an airplane so I won't go into it as I have never done it. I have heard stories of pets suffering and dying on air trips, so do find out all you can about it before you travel. Tell the pilot that your pet is aboard and make sure the plane isn't carrying any radio-active cargo that your pet could be parked on top of or next to. Passenger aircraft frequently carry radioactive material these days, more than we may realize.

On a train trip you can keep your pet with you in a carrying case. We once took a train from Chicago to California and back with our Siamese cat Pooh Bah. We had a stateroom so we could let him out of the case (of course we brought a litter box) It was an easy trip for us as he preferred to stay under the seats for the whole trip.

Whether you travel by plane, train or automobile, or just make trips to the veterinarian, a sturdy, well ventilated carrying case, the best you can find, is a very good investment.

Chicken Scratch. My husband found a new use for this. We and a lot of people who feed birds in the winter, find after while that buying all that bird seed gets quite expensive, especially when the squirrels also show up at the feeder. So we mix it with chicken scratch which is much cheaper and save quite a bit of money. Remember if you do start to feed birds, they depend on you to continue and even being away for a week or so can cause hardship for them, unless you get someone to feed them for you.

Weigh your animal from time to time to see if his food is adequate or if he is getting too much.

Hot Water mixed with cereal food helps the animals' body to absorb minerals from the food and makes the meal more palatable.

Rancid Oils or Fats should *never* be fed to your pet—especially a cat. Cats are very susceptible to a painful disease called steatitus or yellow fat disease which causes disintigration of muscles. If you suspect that your cat has eaten anything rancid, give him some Vitamin E right away. Fats going rancid come from fish that is high, unrefrigerated cod liver oil, wheat germ oil, or seed and nut oils that are not properly preserved.

Whey If your cat or dog gets diarrhea from milk make sure the food you are feeding does not contain whey. Look at the pet food labels.

Raw Foods vs. Cooked Foods. Man is the only creature that cooks his food. While working on this cook book I have come to believe more and more in the value of raw foods. There have been instances of persons who recovered from serious illnesses by eating only uncooked fruits and vegetables. I question whether a diet consisting entirely of foods that are cooked or processed at high temperatures will give your cat or dog the vitamins and enzymes he needs to be healthy all his life.

There have been some experiments with caged cats by Pottenger and Simonsen that have become classic. Several cats were divided into two groups. In cage one, the cats were fed raw meat and raw milk diets. Those in cage two were fed only cooked meat and pasteurized milk. All the cats were pleasantly housed with clean sand floors, running water and a climbing tree. The cats in cage one remained normal, friendly, and raised large families of kittens. In cage two the cats became irritable, fought among themselves, and developed diseases and deficiencies which were never reversed. There were no fourth generation survivors in this second group.

Since most of the cats around eat only cooked food and drink pasteurized milk, and seem to be much better off than the cats in cage two, there must be some other factors at work. Perhaps a loving home or an occasional bite of raw meat or green grass makes a difference. We do know that heat destroys some vitamins, even pasteurization causes deterioration of vitamins B1, C, A, and E. So probably most cats and dogs would be happier and healthier with some raw food every day.

How to Make an Instant Meal Using Raw Foods. I find this to be a healthful and convenient way to fix a meal for my dog and cats.

> 1 lb. beef, beef and liver, kidneys, heart, mutton or chicken backs, necks, wings, gizzards, etc.
>
> ⅓ cup raw millers' bran
>
> ¼ cup wheat germ

133

¼ cup raw minced greens such as parsley,
  dandelion greens, spinach, celery leaves,
  alfalfa sprouts, green peppers, etc.
¼ cup oil or fat if meat is lean
2 tablespoons supplement (page 99)
boiling water

Cut the meat into chunks; if using chicken,
smash the pieces first with a rolling pin to pulverize
the bones. Mix all together and add enough boiling water to give the consistency of gravy. Serve
over biscuits or cereal. The protein content of this
recipe is too high to be used with a high protein
commercial dry food. The first time you make this
dish, mix it with your pet's regular food, using a
small amount at first and increasing it gradually
until he gets used to the new taste. Be patient.

Bran and Bladder Infections. Kiki, my four-
teen-year-old lilac point, spayed female cat,
skinny and bedraggled, had a very distressing
bladder infection. She spent much of her time
squatting on her litter box or looking for a more
secluded corner to leave a few dribbles or a crim-
son spot. She was so fierce in resisting all medicines from the veterinarian, I gave up that struggle.
I tried all the remedies in my book, but she ate very
little. She was a most miserable animal and a
disgrace to me and my work.

Then one day I noticed that there were bugs
in a large bag of raw millers' bran, and to use it up I
sprinkled liberal amounts of it on all pet food every
day. Before it was gone, I saw that Kiki's appetite
had improved and she wasn't spending so much
time on her litter box. What brought about this
miracle? Was it the bran? I looked up the food

elements in bran and found that it does contain moderate amounts of vitamin B6 and magnesium. It might also have been that the animal protein content of her food was too high and using the bran brought it down. Too much meat protein in the diet of a human or an animal is likely to bring on urinary problems.

Kiki now looks like her beautiful self again—a cream and lilac powder puff with great, pale blue eyes. She hasn't had another sick day, and I've not stopped using the bran.

Food Additives and Dog Biting. Some children are so sensitive to food additives and dyes they become behavior problems and are called hyperactive. They are only pleasant to be around after being put on a diet free of all additives and dyes such as the Feingold diet. We do not know that dogs who bite and cats who are nasty are sensitive to additives and dyes, but it is easy to see how much color is added to commercial pet foods—not for the health of the dog or cat of course, but to appeal to the purchaser.

A Word of Caution. If you are using liberal amounts of brewers yeast or powdered skim milk every day, your pet's diet may become unbalanced. Because of its rich phosphorus content, brewers yeast should have calcium and magnesium added to it. Some kinds are sold already mixed, but you can do it yourself by adding to each pound of yeast ½ cup of calcium lactate or $1\frac{1}{2}$ tablespoon of bone meal and 2 tablespoons of magnesium carbonate, oxide or epsom salt.

Skim milk powder should be supplemented

with some fat or oil plus cod liver oil. The reason for this is that vitamins A and D, which are necessary for the digestion and absorption of milk, are fat soluble and found only in cream. As they are absent from skim milk, digesting it robs the body of its store of these vitamins and a severe deficiency can be the result, bringing on night blindness and other problems.

More About Fleas. Fleas are prodigious egg layers. A young couple I know went on vacation one summer leaving their two cats at home. A friend fed them and the cats were able to enter and leave the house by an open window. A cat-hating neighbor took the cats "for a ride" one day, an abominable act, and when my friends returned, their house was free of cats, but black with fleas! They covered the furniture, the carpets, everything. What happened was the thousands of flea eggs that had fallen off the cats and a large dog (who was at a kennel) hatched in the house. Having no bodies to hop on, the fleas infested the furniture.

I read in a *Smithsonian* magazine of a "dear, gentle" lady whose dog had died. Fleas soon took up residence in her Oriental rugs and upholstery. She tried sprays and burning smelly stuff, but to no avail. So she invited the neighborhood children and their dogs to a puppy party. When the children and dogs departed so did the fleas! She doesn't sound so dear, gentle to me. But the story does say something about fleas and how desperate one can get.

You may notice one day in late summer that your pet is shedding black and white "dandruff" that looks like salt and pepper. These are flea eggs and flea feces. Under a magnifying glass the white specks look like white jelly beans and the dark specks are mostly dried blood. The eggs will sooner or later hatch into fleas. This is generally the way they get into your house. They do not hop off your pets.

To get rid of flea eggs, brush your pet over newspaper, then gather the paper up and burn it. Keep your pet's bedding free of eggs by washing it or burning it if necessary. Vacuum your house often and spray your carpets if you see the little critters hopping around. Some people even spray their yards. The main thing is to break up the life cycle before they multiply again.

Talk to Your Animals. If talking to plants helps them to grow and flourish, talking to your pets should be even more rewarding. The human voice has powers we haven't begun to explore. I think we all have experienced this while reassuring a frightened animal or a child by talking or crooning to him.

The main thing is to remember to do it. Some outgoing, cheerful types chat all the time, but many of us must think about it first. I have found singing to be invaluable when trying to get my cat or dog to submit to a brushing or a flea treatment. The song doesn't have to be beautiful or even appropriate, any song will do. I make them up as I go along, usually using a refrain like: "What a marvelous kitty (doggie) you are."

In Conclusion

Always remember that your pet depends on you for love and security and for all his needs. Mealtimes should always be at a regular time and place that he can count on. Don't be haphazard about this, and don't teach your children responsibility at your pet's expense. If feeding your cat or dog is your child's job, see that he does it regularly and try to keep it cheerful. Water should be available at all times.

Your cat being a fastidious animal should have his litter box kept clean, and of course your dog should be able to get outside when he needs to.

Getting to know and appreciate your unique animal is a marvelous experience and he will thrive on the love you give him and return it in his own particular way. Our Weimeraner dog named Duchess, for instance, took on the job of a den mother to the family, being fearlessly protective of us all and insisting on her right always to be next to us on couch or bed. Joe, our neurotic black cat adopted a stray black kitten who appeared at our door one day. He cleaned and cared for her and so enjoyed his new role as a father that he lost his nervous habits. Of course we then had to adopt her and we were never sorry. The two are still the best of friends.

Sometimes I think how simple life would be without any pets at all. But I know too how very dull and incomplete it would be. Animals are not at all concerned with metaphysics or the state of the world or any other intellectual or abstract pursuits, but they have highly developed senses and feelings and these are two qualities we humans would do well to cultivate. They know when we are feeling sad and do their best to comfort us. They love to share our joyous moods as well as our quiet ones, and always make us feel glad when we arrive home. Compared to these things, what care they need is very little. I hope using this book is helpful in providing the kind of care that will bring about a difference in the health and well-being of your pet.

• • •

BIBLIOGRAPHY

Nutrient Requirements of Dogs, Number 8 Revised 1972 National Academy of Sciences

Lets Eat Right to Keep Fit, Adele Davis

Lets Cook It Right, Adele Davis

Diet for a Small Planet, Frances Moore Lappé

The Complete Book of Dog Care. Leon F. Whitney, DVM.

Composition of Foods, Agriculture Handbook No. 8.

The Complete Herbal Book for the Dog, Juliette de Bairacli Levy

Puppy Rearing by Natural Methods, Juliette de Bairacli Levy

The Collins Guide to Dog Nutrition, Donald R. Collins DVM

The Well Dog Book, Terri MiGinnis, DVM

The Well Cat Book, Terri McGinnis, DVM.

The Guide to Nutritional Management of Small Animals, Mark Morris Jr., DVM, MS, PhD.— Stanly M. Teter, DVM.

Feline Dietetics Nutritional Management in Health and Disease, Mark Morris Jr., DVM, MS, PhD.

Canine and Feline Nutritional Requirements, U.F.A.W. Handbook chapter by Patricia Scott.

Nutrient Requirements of Laboratory Animals, No. 10 National Research Council.

The Complete Book of Cat Care. Leon F. Whitney, DVM.

BIBLIOGRAPHY (con'd)

The Nutrition of Cats, Dr. Jim Corbin

Cat Breeding and General Management, P.M. Soderberg

Cats, An Intelligent Owner's Guide, Henderson and Mead

Diseases of the Cat, Wilkinson

Back to Eden, Jethro Kloss

Nutrition Scoreboard, Michael Jacobson, PhD.

Old Fashioned Recipe Book, Carla Emery

American Animal Hospital Association Journal, Paul M. Newberne, DVM., M.Sc., PhD. March and April 1974

Prevention, articles and letters

> *Feed Your Pet Better at Less Cost*, Linda Cressman, January 1974

> *Readers' Best Ideas for Healthier Pets* Oct., 1974

> *More Ideas From Readers for Healthier Pets* Nov., 1974

> *Cats Need A Varied Diet to Keep Healthy*, Lois Stevenson May, 1975

> *What the Pet Food Commercials Don't Tell You*, Lois Stevenson July, 1975

> *A Necklace of Poison*, Robert Bahr August 1975

The Mother Earth News, articles and letters too numerous to mention.

INDEX

Accidents 127
Addiction 11, 89-90, 92
Aging–Diet For An
  Older Animal 79-81
Alfalfa 69, 95, 104, 126
Alfalfa Sprouts 70
Allergy–Diet For 77
Aloe plant 102
American Medical
  Association 91
Amino Acids 13
Anemia 104
Anne's Dog's Dish 65
Antibiotics 12, 101
Appetite 78
Apple Cider Vinegar 98, 103
Apples 11
Arsenic 108
Arteries 10
Arthritis 98
Artichoke, Jerusalem 69
Ascorbic Acid–
  Vitamin C 97-98, 133
Ash 11, 83, 125

Bacon fat 88
Bacteria 12, 108
Balfour, Lady Eve 12
Barley 34
Barley Water 97
Basic Low Calorie Diet 76
Bathing 107
Bauernfruhstuck 54
Beans 13, 44-50
  Beanburgers 49
  Lentil Loaf 50
  Lentil Stew With Rice 49
Beef 59-67, 84
  Anne's Dog's Dish 65
  Beef Heart Meal For Cats
    And Kittens 64
  Beef Kidney 64
  Beef Stew 83
  Meat Loaf 65
  Soy Bean Chili Con
    Carne 66
  Tripe a la Mode de
    Canine 67

Beef Liver 62, 84
  Liver And Oatmeal Dish
    For Cats And Kittens 63
Bee Stings 103
Belfield, Wendell O. 97
Berries 11
Birth Control 118
Biscuits
  Dog Biscuits De Luxe 40
  Hard Biscuits For Dogs
    And Cats 39
Blackberry Leaves 72, 102,
  103
Bladder 81-86
Bland Diet For Pet With
  Food Allergy 77
Blood 82
Boiled Squid 58
Bone Meal 96, 111
Bones 20, 88, 115
  Marrow Bones 20
Bran 33, 96, 104, 107, 126, 134
Bread
  Cornbread 42
Brewers Yeast 13, 17, 94,
  106, 111
Broccoli 69, 71
Bronchitis 104
Buckwheat 26, 34
Bugs 33
Burns 102
Buttermilk 51, 52
  Buttermilk Breakfast 53
  Buttermilk Stew 53
By-products 89

Cake
  Carob Cakes 42
  Carrot Peanut Cake 74
  Cat And Dog Cakes or
    Petah 41
  Johnny Cake 43
Calcium 18, 87, 94
Calories 17
  Basic Low Calorie Diet 76
Camomile 72
Carbohydrates 15, 90
Carob 42, 104, 126

143

Carob Cakes 42
Carrots 9, 70
Carrot Peanut Cake 74
Castration 82, 118
Cat And Dog Cakes or
    Petah 41
Catfish Pie 74
Cauliflower 71
Celery 71
Cereals 13, 24-25, 32-35,
    50, 93
    Corn Meal Mush 34
    Five Grain Cereal 35
    Three Grain Cereal 35
    Unground Wheat Cereal
        33
    Very Cheap Cereal For
        Dogs 24
    Very Cheap Cereal With
        Meat 25
    Whole Wheat Cereal 32
    Whole Wheat Mush 32
Cheese 53-54
Chemicals 10
Chicken 20
    Chicken Heads 68
    Chicken Loaf 25
    Chicken Neck Stew With
        Giblets 68
    Chicken Stew 83
Chicken Scratch 24, 25, 26,
    131
Children 133
Chili Powder 66
Cholesterol 96
Cod Liver Oil 94, 100,
    112, 115, 116
Colds 104
Collards 69
Collins, Donald R. 17, 62,
    88, 91-92
Comfrey 72
Commercial Pet Foods 87-92
Compost 126-127
Constipation 104
Cooked Whole Soybeans 45
Cookies—Kitty Catnip
    Cookies 40
Corbin, Jim 125
Corn 49

Corn Bread 42
Corn Chapatties 43
Corn Meal 33, 107
Corn Meal Mush 34
Crackers 38-43
    Oatmeal Crisps 38
    Rye Crisps 38
    Vitamin Crisps 38
    Wheat Crisps 38
Crunchies
    Doggie Crunchies 26
    Kitty Or Doggie
        Crunchies I 28
    Doggie And Kitty
        Crunchies II 30
    Doggie And Kitty
        Crunchies III 31

Dandelions 71
Davis, Adele 82
Diarrhea 78, 111
Diets 75-86
    Basic Low Calorie
        Diet 76
    Bland Diet For Pet With
        Food Allergy 77
    Diet For An Older
        Animal 79
    Diet To Relieve Urinary
        Obstruction 83
    Foods For A Low
        Sodium Diet 77
Digestive Problems 104
Digestive Tract 101
Dinner For An Older Cat 81
Disease—See Illness
Dishes 128
Dog Biscuits De Luxe 40
Dry Food—Commercial 88
Dry Food 28
    Doggie Crunchies 26
    Kitty Or Doggie
        Crunches I 28
    Doggie And Kitty
        Crunchies II 30
    Doggie And Kitty
        Crunchies III 31
Dry Shampoo 107

Eczema 98, 103

Eggs 54, 115
  Bauernfruhstuck 54
  Egg Drop Soup 54
  Egg Nog 54
  Salmon Egg Foo Yung 55
  Scrambled Eggs And
    Liver 55
  Scrambled Eggs And
    Sardines 55
Egg Shells 54
Egg Whites 54
Energy 8
Epsom Salts 96, 111
Esbilac 112
Eucalyptus 104
Eye Rims 102
Eyes 103

Fasting 78, 102
Fats 14, 88
Fiber 11, 104, 126
First Aid 101
Fish 57-59
  Boiled Squid 58
  Catfish Pie 74
  Clam Chowder 59
  Fishhead Stew Or
    Mehitabel's
    Bouillabaise 23
  Kitty Potato Fish Dish 58
  Party Mackerel Or
    Salmon Loaf 73
  Salmon Egg Foo Yung 55
  Scrambled Eggs And
    Sardines 55
  Smelts 58-59
  Tuna Or Mackerel
    Patties 58
Five Grain Cereal 35
Flax Seed 104
Fleas 105-107, 108, 136-137
Flour 32, 33
Folic Acid 62
Folk Medicine–Dr. Jarvis 98
Foods For A Low Sodium
  Diet 77
Food Supplements 93-100
Formula For Puppies 112
Formula For Kittens 116
Fruit 11

Garlic 71, 104, 106, 107,
  108, 111, 115
Gas 101
General Formula For An
  Older Dog's Dinner 80
Geriatric Vitamin Mix 81
Gô 46
Goats 51
Golden Seal 103, 104
Grains 13, 16, 32-35, 50, 93
Grass 12, 69-70, 85
Greens 69, 70, 86
Grits–Soy Grits Cereal 46
Growth 18

Hard Biscuits For Dogs
  And Cats 39
Heart–Beef Heart 64
Hearts 95, 96
Heartworm 108-109
Hemorrhage 109
Herbs 69-72, 102
Homemade Soy Grits 45
Honey 86, 102
House Plants 69
Hush Puppies 43

Illness 97, 101
Insect Bites 103
Iodine 95
Iron 104

Jacobson, Michael 62, 69
Jerusalem Artichoke 69
Johnny Cake 43
Joints 94
Jones, Dorothea Van
  Grundy 44

Kale 69
Kaopectate 104
Kasha 36
Kelp 71, 95, 100
Kloss, Jethro 103
Kidney–Beef Kidney 64
Kidneys 86, 125
Kidney Stones 83, 125
Kitty And Doggy Pot Au Feu
  21
Kitty Catnip Cookies 40

Kitty Potato Fish Dish 58

Lactation 95
Lactic Acid 51
Lactose 51
Lappé. Frances Moore 16
Lasagna 66
  Meatless Lasagna 56
Laxative 104
Lead toxicity 91
Lecithin 96
Leftovers 26-28
Lentils 48
  Lentil Stew With Rice 49
  Lentil Loaf 50
Levy, Juliette de Bairacli 11,
  12, 51, 59, 62, 71, 78, 85,
  86, 102, 113-114
Lice 98
Liver 62. 104
  Scrambled Eggs And
    Liver 55
Liver and Oatmeal Dish For
  Cats And Kittens 63
Liver Sausage 55
Litter 126, 127, 133

Magnesium 82, 96, 111, 115
Manure 11
Marjoram 72
Marrow Bones 20
Meat 14, 16, 18, 59-67, 132
Meatless Lasagna 56
Meat Loaf 65
Melons 11
Milk 10, 51, 117, 132
Millet 34
Minerals 15, 82, 83, 93, 99,
  111, 125
Mint 71, 72
Molasses 104
Mold 12, 54
Morris, Mark 75, 83
Mosquitos 108-109
Mother Hubbards Soup
  Bone Stock 20
Mush
  Cornmeal Mush 34
  Whole Wheat Mush 32
Myrrh 103, 104

Names For Pets 119-124
Natural Rearing 51, 60, 102
Nerves 94
Nettles 72
Nutrition 13-16
Nutrients 15
Nutrition Scoreboard 62, 69

Oatmeal 34, 107
  Liver and Oatmeal 63
  Milk Of Oats 97
Oatmeal Crisps 38
Odors—Doggie Odors 99
Oils 88
Overweight 76
Onions 71

Pain 94
Parsley 71, 72, 86
Party Mackerel Or
  Salmon Loaf 73
Peas 71
Peat Moss 126
Penny Royal 106
Peppermint 72
Petah 41
Pet Foods—How To Use Com-
  mercial Pet Foods 87-92
Phosphorus 18, 87-88
Pie—Catfish Pie 74
Pills 130
Popcorn 77
Potassium 96
Potato 70
Potato Chips 77
Pottenger And Simonsen 132
Poultry
  Chicken Heads 68
  Chicken Loaf 25
  Chicken Neck Stew With
    Giblets 68
  Chicken Stew 83
Pregnancy 111-117
Preservatives 90
Pretzels 77
Proportions Of Food Elements
  For Dogs And Cats 14
Propylene Glycol 90
Protein 13-14, 16, 24

146

Putrefaction 101
Pyrethrum 105

Rancidity 10, 57, 88,
    95, 132
Raspberry Leaves 72, 104
Rashes 98, 103
Raw Meal, Instant, 133-134
Red Clover 72, 103
Rice 34
Ringworm 103
Ritz Diet To Relieve Urinary
    Obstruction 83
Rose Hips 98
Rosemary 102
Rotenone 106
Rye Crisps 38

Sage 72, 115
Salad 27
Salmon Egg Foo Yung 55
Salt 77
Savory 72
Sawdust 126-127
Scrambled Eggs And
    Liver 55
Scrambled Eggs And
    Sardines 55
Scrapple 37
Sea Salt 100
Seaweed 71
Sedative 94
Seeds 16, 40
Semi-Moist Foods 89-90, 92
Shurtleff And Aoyagi 46
Shopping Day Stock 22
Sickness 97, 101
Slippery Elm 71
Smelts 58-59
Snacks 84
Soap—Flea Soap 107
Soderberg, P. M. 129
Soup
    Clam Chowder 59
    Fish Head Stew or
        Mehitabel's
        Bouillabaise 23
    Kitty And Doggy Pot
        Au Feu 21
    Mother Hubbards Soup
        Bone Stock 20

Shopping Day Stock 22
Soybeans 13, 44-48
    Cooked Whole Soybeans
        45
    Homemade Soy Grits 45
    Soy Grits Cereal 46
    Soy Loaf 46
    Soy Patties 47
Soy Bean Chili Con Carne 66
Soy Bean Milk, I, II and III 47-48
Soy Flour 44
Soy Grits 44, 45
Soy Powder 44
Squid, Boiled 58
Starch 36
Steatitus 57, 132
Stews
    Beef Stew 83
    Buttermilk Stew 53
    Chicken Neck Stew With
        Giblets 68
    Chicken Stew 83
Sugar 90

Teeth 90
Three Grain Cereal 35
Thyme 72
Thyroid Gland 95
Ticks 107
Tomato 71
Toxins 91
Traveling 130
Tree Bark 71
Tripe a la Mode de Canine 67
Trout 84
Tuna or Mackerel Patties 58
Turnips 70

Unground Wheat Cereal 33
Urinary Problems 81, 86

Vegetable 68-71, 84
Vegetable Proteins 13, 16
Vitamin Crisps 38
Vitamins 51, 93, 99, 133
Vitamin A 69, 94, 102, 133
Vitamin B1 Thiamine 57, 60,
    61, 106, 133
Vitamin B6 Pyridoxine 60-
    61, 125

Vitamin C Ascorbic Acid 97, 98, 133
Vitamin D 94
Vitamin E 57, 95, 100, 102, 133
Vitamin K 95
Vomiting 78
Vinegar 98, 103

Wastes, Body 117
Water 82, 132
Watercress 71
Weight 76, 131
Welsh "Rabbit" 56
Wheat Cereal 32-33
Wheat Crisps 38

Wheat Germ 13, 33, 95
Whey 132
Whole Grains 93, 115
Whole Wheat Cereal 32
Whole Wheat Mush 32
Witch Hazel 102, 107
Worms 98, 107, 111
    Heartworm 108
Wounds 99, 102

Yeast 13, 17, 94, 106
Yogurt 51, 101
    Easy Yogurt 53
    Yogurt Youthtail 52

Zinc 98-99